Let's PLaY!

100
Popular Games
for Children

Shelalagh McGovern

ROCKPOOL
PUBLISHING

We are in our truest form when playing a game and it is such a
joy to live in the moment and to play.

Dedication
To Chris and Billy for the games we play everyday.

A Rockpool book
Published by Rockpool Publishing
24 Constitution Road, Dulwich Hill, NSW 2203, Australia
www.rockpoolpublishing.com.au

First published in 2010
Copyright © Shelalagh McGovern, 2010

National Library of Australia Cataloguing-in-Publication entry

Let's play : 100 popular games for kids / Shelalagh
McGovern ; photographs by Stephen Reinhardt.

1st ed.
9781921295348 (pbk.)
Games.
Reinhardt, Stephen.
790.1922

Cover and internal design by Ellie Exarchos
Typeset by Ice Cold Publishing
Printed and bound by Everbest Printing Co Ltd, China
10 9 8 7 6 5 4 3 2 1

'Some of the games described in this book are Theatre sports games. These games are copyright
Lyn Pearce and appear in more detail in Improvisation; The Guide. They are used with permission of
the publishers. The games are: 75. Knife and fork, 76. Postcards, 78. Expert double figures.

About the author

Shelalagh McGovern is passionate about aerial and circus arts. She co-founded Aerialize - Sydney Aerial Theatre in 1998 and was the Director until 2008. She is an aerial instructor and performer with over 12 years experience and a background in gymnastics. She trained in aerial skills with trainers from Circus Oz, Flying Fruit Fly Circus, Legs on the Wall and Circus Space, London. Some of her aerial highlights include performing with Les Comediens, the Flying Lotahs in Singapore and in the Sydney Olympic Games Opening Ceremony.

Shelalagh has directed aerial segments for the Schools Spectacular and Sydney Youth Olympics opening Ceremony as well as many Aerialize productions. She produced and co-directed Walking on Air, an aerial-rock performance for the Studio, Sydney Opera House.

She has a Bachelor of Arts from the University of NSW, a graduate certificate in Arts Administration from UTS and is a qualified rigger. She lives in Sydney with her husband and son.

Acknowledgements

I'd like to thank the people who I have played games with over the years, including the performers, instructors and directors for their generosity and creativity as well as the students who I have taught, for their enthusiasm, and shared enjoyment of the games we have played.

Thanks to the playful children (and their parents) who appear in this book; Stella, Sarah, Jordan, India, Ella, Alison, Victoria, Sanne, Tom, Luuk, Saffron, Ruby, Nicholas, Chealsea, Lincoln, Isabella, Rhiana, Kane and Angus. Many thanks also to Jess Paraha, and to my nieces and nephews (and especially their parents) who also appear in this book. Thanks to Lyn Pierce for her permission to use Theatre sport games in this book and to Stephen for the photography.

Finally, thanks to my publisher Lisa, for asking me to write this book.

Contents

GAMES FOR 5–6 YEAR OLDS
ICEBREAKER GAMES

LIVELY AND PHYSICAL GAMES

THEATRICAL AND TRUST GAMES

WORD GAMES FOR A GROUP

CLASSIC GAMES

GAMES FOR 7–9 YEAR OLDS
ICEBREAKER GAMES

LIVELY AND PHYSICAL GAMES

THEATRICAL GAMES

TRUST GAMES

WORD GAMES FOR A GROUP

SKIPPING AND BALL GAMES
SKIPPING

BALL GAMES

GAME COMBINATIONS FOR GROUPS OF PLAYERS

Introduction

Kids love to play! There's nothing quite like playing a game. When you play a game well, it becomes your whole world and nothing else exists. You interact, communicate and laugh with others. Children are particularly good at playing games because they live in the moment. We learn best when we enjoy what we are doing and in an environment where we can express ourselves, make mistakes and be creative.

As an adult I still love to play games. For over 10 years, I have taught circus, aerial and drama skills to children and adults from 5 to 70 years old from complete beginners to professional performers. I have used games to begin a class, help students work together and to develop performances.

One of the best things about playing games is having fun. Games can cross cultural, social, language and age barriers. Playing games at parties and events creates an opportunity for people to enjoy themselves while getting to know one another.

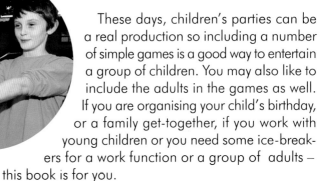

These days, children's parties can be a real production so including a number of simple games is a good way to entertain a group of children. You may also like to include the adults in the games as well. If you are organising your child's birthday, or a family get-together, if you work with young children or you need some ice-breakers for a work function or a group of adults – this book is for you.

I have compiled a collection of tried and tested games that I have enjoyed with many people. Although they are set out in age categories, this is only a guide as most of these games can be played by anyone, no matter what their age. The main objective is to have fun.

Ready, set, go – getting started

Leading the games

If you are leading the games be a confident and fair leader. Make sure you understand the rules of the games. Ask a family member or friend to assist you with running the games. Always take time to explain the game and make sure the players understand how to play. You will need to physically demonstrate actions when explaining some of the games listed.

Kids love to ask why or offer suggestions. Be ready to explain why and allow for variations to evolve. A child might suggest playing the game a new way. Try the child's suggestion if it is appropriate, and embrace their ideas if they are practical for the whole group.

Listen to the group and watch them play. Always finish a game while everyone is having fun. That way you can go back to it again with ease. Most of the games in this book are crowd-pleasers, but each group is different and group dynamics can change quickly so be ready to let something go if it's not working.

Give your players responsibilities and decision-making opportunities. Empowering your players will bring out the best in them, so try to choose a range of games that cater for the different strengths of the players in the group. Some will be good at physical games while others may excel at memory games. You may like to show the book to the players and encourage them to choose and lead the games they like.

Safety first

Do your utmost to create a safe and fun environment so the players feel comfortable with the games. At the beginning of a session go through key safety rules together. Encourage the players to be responsible for their actions, respect their fellow players and the environment they are in.

As the leader, remember that some of the players may be confused or overwhelmed with too much information or high expectations. Others may just be really excited and ready to play. Start with fun and easy games to build confidence, trust and teamwork, and then proceed to more complicated games. Generally all players want to fit in and belong to the group so they may be distressed if they can't for some reason. Players who are bored thrive when given decision-making opportunities. For example 'Rock, paper, scissors' is a good game to allow natural leaders to shine.

Some of the games in this book are competitive so teach the players to play fairly and with compassion for their team members. As the leader, place the emphasis on playing the game rather than the outcome.

Play the games in large open spaces and clear any obstructions in the play area. To avoid accidents, anticipate problems. If the players are over-excited, stop the game and change to a quiet game that will help them to re-focus.

It is advisable to have a first-aid kit on hand and for the leader of the games to have some first-aid knowledge.

How to use this book

Criteria

All the criteria are listed at the beginning of each game and are a guide only. The time taken to play each game will change depending on the size of the group. Once you know the games well you can play many of them across the different age groups. Most of the games in this book work best with 10 or more players but a range of them can be played with less.

Icebreaker games

Begin your party or session with some icebreaker games. Choose one or two that you like for each session. Starting a session in a circle allows the group to see one another and become more familiar. It also helps to build group confidence. All these games are best played with a group of around 10 or more players, but they can be played with less as I have indicated.

Lively and physical games

These games are very active, lots of fun and require a good amount of space as they involve running and chasing. Be sure to create the boundaries and explain the rules properly. Watch how everyone is interacting and stop the game if it begins to look too chaotic.

Theatrical and trust games

Theatrical and trust games are best played at the end of a session, once the group has had time together. These games encourage the players to be creative and think quickly. They help players to explore ideas and express themselves theatrically.

Quieter games

The quieter games are good to play when the group needs to re-focus. They are great for playing indoors, in a small room or on a scorching hot or rainy day. These games can be played in smaller groups.

Classics

You would have played these classic games once upon a time but you may have forgotten about them or exactly how to play them. These are fun games that you will use now and again. They are traditional games that most people know, so everyone can join in and they won't need much explanation.

Tips
* Be positive and supportive of the players at all times.
* Encourage full participation, teamwork, fair play and compassion.
* Always stop a game while everyone is having fun.
* Give players responsibilities and ownership of the games.
* Be creative with the games and make variations of your own.
* Although a goal is important, focus on 'playing' the game rather than the winner.
* Play safe and have fun!

Games for 5–6 year olds

1. Colour and action

Age range: 5–6
Players: 5 or more
Playing time: 5–10 minutes
Formation: Start standing randomly in the space.
Space: Both small and large, indoors or outdoors

How to play

The group selects a number of colours and gives each colour an action (see the examples below). All players do the action when the colour is called out. The leader begins by matching one colour with an action. For example, the leader calls out 'RED' and 'turn around on the spot'. So the action for the colour red is to turn around on the spot.

The leader asks a player to select a different colour and perform an action to go with it. They may say 'BLUE' and 'stand on one foot'. The leader calls out 'BLUE' and everyone must stand on one foot. The leader goes through the group inviting players to choose about 7 colours with matching actions. Allow the group time to practise these.

Play by elimination. The leader randomly calls out the different colours and players have to do the action as quickly as possible. Anyone who does the wrong action or is too slow is asked to sit out. The winner is the last player left.

Variation

The leader can nominate the first round of colours and actions for the game if the children are too shy.

Example

Some examples for colour and actions are:

Yellow – Jump up and down three times.
Green – Lie on your back.
Orange – Sit cross-legged on the floor.
Purple – Wiggle your hips.
Brown – Three star jumps.
Aqua – A karate kick.

2. Touch that!

Age range: 5–6
Players: 5 or more
Set up time: 1 minute
Playing time: 5–6 minutes
Space: Anywhere in the space.

How to play

Tell the players that you will call out names of things and when you do they must run over and touch that object. For example, you call out 'touch the floor' and the children all touch the floor. You call out 'touch something red' and the children must find something red to touch. Call out 'touch the door' and the children run over and all place their hands on the door.

Increase the speed of your commands as they become familiar with the game. Eliminate players who are the last to do the task each time. The game ends when there is only one player left. Try a few practice runs to get children used to the game.

This game can also be played without eliminations as a warm-up exercise before you move to the main games.

3. Pass the hoop

Age range: 5–6
Players: 5 or more
Set up time: 1–2 minutes
Playing time: 5–6 minutes
Materials: A hoop about 1 metre in diameter
Formation: Players stand in a circle holding hands.
Space: Big enough for all the players to stand in a circle

How to play

All players stand in a circle holding hands. Two people let go of their grip long enough for the leader to place a hoop between their hands and then re-join their hands. The hoop rests over the held hands. The team task is to pass the hoop around the circle in one direction until it returns to the starting point, without letting go of each other's hands.

Once the first hoop is in motion, add a few more hoops to the circle. They should go in the same direction as the first hoop.

19

4. One to ten

Age range: 5–6
Players: 5 or more
Set up time: 1 minute
Playing time: 5–6 minutes
Formation: Sitting randomly in the space.
Space: Can be played in a small space.

How to play

The group spreads out and sits down. The leader says: 'the first instruction is to high five someone'. On the word 'One' the players jump up and high five someone then sit down.

The leader then builds on the instructions. The leader says 'the second instruction is to touch the ground with your elbow. On the word 'Two' players high five someone then touch the ground with their elbow. Continue to add an instruction with a number until you reach ten. Each time you call a new number the children must perform the series of actions beginning from action number One and finishing with the last action added. Some children may find remembering ten commands confusing, so just choose five.

Variation

Some examples of commands:

One – High five someone.

Two – Touch the ground with your elbow.

Three – Lie down on your back and put your feet in the air.

Four – Clap your hands four times.

Five – Shake hands with someone.

Six – Turn around on the spot.

Seven – Crawl between someone's legs.

Eight – Link hands with someone and spin around.

Nine – Lie on your tummy.

Ten – Do a star jump and shout hurrah!

5. Who is it?

Age range: 5–6
Players: 5 or more
Set up time: 1 minute
Playing time: 5–10 minutes
Formation: In a circle.
Space: Indoors in a small space.

How to play

All the players stand in a circle. The leader secretly thinks of one person. The players then ask 'Yes' or 'No' questions. For example, 'Is it a boy?' If the answer is 'No', all in that category (all boys) sit down. All the kids can ask questions, even if they're sitting down. Continue until the children figure out who you secretly picked. Repeat a few times.

22

6. Duck, duck, goose

Age range: 5–6
Players: 8 or more.
Set up time: 2 minutes
Playing time: 5–10 minutes
Formation: Circle
Space: Ensure there is room around the outside of the circle for the players to run.

How to play

At the start of the game you will need to indicate the direction the children will run around the circle. One player is the fox. The rest of the players sit in a circle facing in. The fox walks around the outside of the circle tapping each player on the head calling them a 'duck'. At any point the fox can decide to tap a player on their head and call them a 'goose'. The goose must then stand up and chase the fox around the circle. The fox runs as quickly as possible to get back to the spot where the goose was sitting without being tipped. If the fox succeeds, then the goose becomes the fox and the game begins again. If the goose succeeds in tipping the fox the goose then becomes the fox and the fox must sit in the middle of the circle until someone else is tipped.

Variation

Choose different categories. Many children like 'toilet', 'toilet', 'flush'.

7. Stuck in the mud

Age range: 5 and up
Players: 4 or more
Setup time: 2 minutes
Playing time: 5–15 minutes
Formation: Scattered running
Space: An area 10 by 10 metres. Best played on grass, mats or carpet. Not great on concrete as will be hard on the players' knees—use one of the variations if on a hard surface.

How to play

Select one person to be in. All the other players scatter in the space. The person who is in must run around and tip as many people as he can. When tipped, the player must freeze and stand with their legs apart. The only way they can be freed is for a non-tagged player to crawl under their legs. Players are safe while crawling under legs and cannot be tipped when in that position. The game ends when all players are tipped and therefore frozen. If the games has gone on for a while and the person who is in appears to be tiring, nominate another person or persons to be in with them. This will speed the game up.

Hug in the mud

Instead of crawling under the player's legs to free them, the players give each other a hug to free one another. Whilst in the hug position they cannot be tipped.

Variation

Aeroplanes in the mud

Instead of crawling under the players legs the players run under each outstretched arm (aeroplane wing) respectively to free one another other.

27

8. River, bank, bridge

Age range: 5 and up
Players: 4 or more
Setup time: 2 minutes
Playing time: 5–15 minutes
Formation: Scattered running
Space: An area 10 by 10 metres.

How to play

Ask the players to stand on one side of a line. In this position they are standing on the 'bank' of the river. When you call out 'river', they are to jump over the line into the river. When you call 'bank' they jump back to where they started. When you call 'bridge' they must jump and turn sideways landing with their legs straddled either side of the line. They can face either left or right.

Randomly call out 'bank', 'river' and 'bridge'. The players must move as quickly as possible to each command. You can confuse the players by calling bank when they are still on the bank, if a player jumps or overbalances into the river they are out. A player is out if they do the wrong move to any of the commands. Add extra commands to the game once they are familiar with the first three. Following is a list of extra commands and their actions. Physically demonstrate the extra commands to the children before adding them. This game is quick to explain and play and kids love it.

The commands and actions

The commands and actions are as follows:

Bank – Standing on the starting side of the line.

River – Standing on the opposite side to the bank.

Bridge – Standing with both legs either side of the line facing sideways.

Harbour Bridge – Place your hands on one side of the line and legs on the other with arms and legs straight, push your hips up to create the shape of a bridge with your body.

Crocodile – Lie across the line on your tummy with your arms outstretched to make a snapping motion like the jaws of a crocodile.

Frog – Squat down with your knees apart and place your hands on the ground in the position of a frog. (This is done on the bank side.)

9. Red light, green light

Age range: 5–6
Players: 10 or more.
Set up time: 1–2 minutes
Playing time: 5–10 minutes
Formation: This game involves the group running forward in a line.
Space: A long open space to accommodate the children running.

How to play

One player is the traffic light. All the other players stand in line about 10 metres away from the traffic light. To begin play, the traffic light faces away from the group and says 'green light'. The others then creep, walk or run while the traffic light's back is turned.

At any time the traffic light can call 'red light' and turn around. The players must freeze. If the traffic light catches a player moving then they are sent back to the start. Play continues when the traffic light turns back around and says 'green light'. Players who are sent back to the start stay in the game.

The first player to touch the traffic light on the back wins the game and becomes the traffic light for the next game.

This is a physical game that involves running, sneaking and freezing. Kids love it.

The traffic light does not call out 'red light' or 'green light', they simply turn their head. Any player they see moving must go back to the start.

Variation

In pairs, link arms. Pairs creep forward with their arms linked and must freeze together when the traffic light turns around. If one player moves they both have to go back to the start.

10. Octopus

Age range: 5–6

Players: 10 or more

Set up time: About 5 minutes. Divide the playing area into two safe zones about 10 metres apart by drawing two lines or using markers behind which the safe zone will be.

Playing time: 5–15 minutes

Formation: Scattered running.

Space: A large area of 10 by 10 metres.

How to play

Everyone begins the game as a fish and stands in one of the safe zones on one side of the space. One person is the Octopus and he stands in the middle of the playing area, between the safe zones. Play begins when the Octopus calls out, 'Little fish, little fish, come swim in my ocean!'

All players must cross the space without being tipped by the Octopus. The Octopus chases and tips as many 'fish' as possible within the playing field but not in the safe zones. Anyone who is tipped must sit down where they are. They become the octopus tentacles and tip the fish from where they are sitting as they run across the playing area. Once the players get to the other side, the Octopus calls out 'Come swim in my ocean!' and the players run back again. Anyone who runs within arm's reach of the sitting players and gets tipped must sit down.

As the Octopus gains more tentacles it becomes harder for the fish to cross. Play continues until all the fish become tentacles and there is only one fish left.

Variation

For a longer game, allow the tentacles to become fish again once they have tipped someone else. In this case, choose when to stop the game as everyone won't get out.

Variation

Instead of calling 'Little fish, come swim in my ocean', the Octopus can call out categories based on items such as clothing, hair and height. The players in those categories must cross. Category suggestions can be: 'Everyone wearing blue must cross'; 'Everyone with short hair must cross'; 'Everyone wearing shorts must cross', and so on. Players who are tipped still sit down where they are caught and try to tip the other players as they run across.

Variation

When the Octopus tips a player they must join hands with the Octopus. That player now helps tip the fish with their free hand. The other players have to get past the growing octopus without being tipped or encircled. Once the octopus has linked arms with more than two people he or she can no longer tip other players as their hands are joined. Only the players on the end of the chain with their hands free are able to tip other players. Players can run through the middle of the chain so long as they steer clear of the hands of the two players on the end. The chain of an octopus tentacle can encircle a player but only the free hands of the two people on the ends can tip another player.

II. Fruit salad

Age range: 5– 6
Players: 8 or more
Set up time: 2 minutes
Playing time: 5–10 minutes
Formation: Chairs are placed in a circle facing in. If you don't have enough chairs you can play sitting in a circle.
Space: This can be played in a relative small space.
Materials: A number of chairs.

How to play

Have one fewer chairs in the space than the number of players. Nominate a player to be in. Divide players into 3 groups of fruit by going around the circle and naming them either apple, orange or pear. Allocate to the person who is in a fruit name too.

The player who is in stands in the centre of the circle. He calls the name of a fruit. If he calls out apples, everyone who is that fruit must get up quickly and change places. Players who are not apples remain seated. The person in the middle tries to sit in an empty spot whenever players swap positions. If they manage to sit in a chair, the player not sitting in a chair is then in. The person in the middle can also call 'fruit salad' and everyone has to change spots.

Players may not swap seats with someone to their immediate right or left.

Variation

You may choose any category the group likes, such as names of countries, seas, breeds of dogs and so on.

Variation

Ask the player who is in to choose whatever category he likes as long as it identifies more than one person in the group. They may swap with the person on their right or left if they have no other option.

Note

Categories might be:
* ★ Anyone who has short hair.
* ★ Anyone who is wearing a watch.
* ★ Anyone who is wearing the colour blue.
* ★ Anyone who has a brother.
* ★ Calling out 'Fruit Salad' still means that the whole group must stand up and swap places.

12. Chain tip

Age range: 5–6
Players: 6 or more
Set up time: 1 minute
Playing time: 5–10 minutes
Formation: Running within the play boundaries.
Space: A large area of around 10 by 10 metres

How to play

One person is in. He chases all the other players. When he tips a player that player must join hands with the person who is in. The pair continues to chase other players. They tip other players using their free hands. When they tip someone, that person joins them by holding hands. Play until all players have formed a chain. If the last few players are difficult to catch the chain may encircle them.

13. Snake Rope

Age range: 5–6
Players: 8 or more
Set up time: 1 minute
Playing time: 3–7 minutes
Formation: Jumping over a moving rope one at a time
Space: Outdoors or in a large room/hall.
Materials: A length of rope around 8 metres long or more.

How to play

Lay the rope straight on the ground in the middle of a space so that there is room either side. Two persons hold the rope at either end. All the players stand on one side of the rope. The rope holders begin to move the rope backwards and forwards like a snake wiggling, while keeping it flat to the ground. One at a time, players must jump over the rope without it touching any part of their body.

To increase the difficultly rope holders make bigger, more extreme wiggles of the rope. If a player touches the rope while jumping over it he must sit out. The last one to be hit by the rope wins.

14. Balloon tennis

Age range: 5–6
Players: 2 or more
Set up time: 2–3 minutes
Playing time: 3–7 minutes
Formation: Two players face one another.
Space: Inside in a room/hall as the wind will carry the balloons away outside.
Materials: Racquets and a balloon for each pair.

How to play

Players form pairs. Give each player a squash/badminton or toy racquet and a balloon. Pairs hit the balloon to one another across the space using their rackets. If you don't have a racquet players can just use their hands. No need to keep score.

15. Follow the leader

Age range: 5–6
Players: 5 or more
Set up time: Under a minute
Playing time: 2–5 minutes
Formation: In a line or circle.
Space: Played both indoors and outdoors.

How to play

One person is the leader. Everyone lines up behind the leader. The leader starts an action while moving around the room and everyone follows. Walk the way they walk, make the same motions, say the same things, and so on. The leader changes the action frequently. After a minute or so the leader goes to the back of the line and the player behind him be-comes the new leader. Play finishes when everyone has had a go at lead-ing. This exercise does not have to be done in a line, and the leader can simply point to a new leader (who has yet to have a turn) to mix it up. The superviser can call out when the leader has to change or each leader can decide when to hand over the lead.

Variation

In a circle

Stand in a circle. The leader starts a continuous movement and the others copy. For example, the leader may begin by waving his right hand. The whole group then waves to each other. The leader then changes the action to hopping on one foot. All the players must follow. After a few different moves, then pass leadership to another player by pointing to them. The new leader continues with the current movement and then changes the movement. Play continues until everyone in the group has had a go. Players may use sounds, words and facial expressions with their movement.

16. Musical statues

Age range: 5–6
Players: 5 or more
Set up time: 2 minutes
Playing time: 5–10 minutes
Formation: Random
Space: Can be played in a small space.
Materials: Music, preferably lively tracks that are good to dance to.

How to play

Start the music. Players dance or run around the space dancing to the music. They can also jump, skip, hop, etc. When the music stops all the players must freeze like a statue. They stay in their 'frozen' position until the music starts again. Any player who moves or giggles when the music is not playing is out. Continue until there is one player left.

Dance directions

To make the game more lively, give the children dance instructions each time you start the music such as 'this time dance with your right elbow' or 'dance with your left knee'. They will still have to freeze when the music stops but the positions they freeze in will be more interesting and harder to hold.

Variation

Directions for when the music stops

When the music stops the players sit on the floor as quickly as possible. The last player to sit down is out. Change the directive each time and call out what they must do when the music stops before you start the music. Such as, 'this time, lie on your tummy', 'sit on your hands', 'stand on one foot', 'lie on your back', etc. The players who do the wrong movement when the music stops are out.

17. Hello!

Age range: 5–6
Players: 5 or more
Set up time: 1 minute
Playing time: 2–5 minutes
Formation: Seated in a group.
Space: Can be played in a small space.

How to play

Ask one child to sit away from the group with their back to the rest of the children. That person is in. Secretly pick someone in the group to say 'Hello, and the name of the person who is in. Suggest that they use a different voice when addressing the person with their back turned. The player with their back turned has to guess who is addressing them. If they get it right the person who addressed them is in. If they get it wrong, choose another player to address them. Play this a number of times so that all the kids get a go.

18. Ha ha ha

Age range: 5–6
Players: 5 or more
Set up time: 1 minute
Playing time: 3–5 minutes
Formation: Each child lies with their head on another child's stomach.
Space: Indoors, in a small space.

How to play

The children lie on their back with their head's on another person's stomach in a loose ring. On the word 'go', the first person shouts 'Ha' and this is repeated one by one around the group. When you do this everyone's heads bounce up on the person's stomach and it might make some of the children giggle.

Once you get back to the beginning, the first player shouts 'Ha Ha' and the game goes around again. Continue doing this and increase the number of 'Has'. See if you can get to 10 without everyone cracking up with laughter.

19. What am I?

Age range: 5–6
Players: 5 or more
Set up time: 2–3 minutes
Playing time: 5–15 minutes
Formation: Sitting in a circle, facing inwards.
Space: Indoors, in a small space.
Materials: Post-it notes, pen

How to play

Give each player a post-it note and a pen. Ask them to write a noun on it and keep this hidden from everyone else. Some examples are dog, table, book, light, and so on. The players place the post-it note on the forehead of the person on their left.

Taking turns, the children have to ask the group 'Yes' or 'No' questions about who or what they are. Players can only answer with 'Yes' or 'No'. Each child can ask three questions then it's the next person's turn. Continue until all players have guessed what they are. The first person to guess wins but they stay in the game to answer questions of the other players. Some examples of 'Yes' and 'No' questions are Am I alive? Am I in the room? Am I made of wood?

To save time, or if you have a large group divide the players into pairs and play.

20. Chinese whispers

Age range: 5–6
Players: 5 or more
Set up time: 1 minute
Playing time: 5–10 minutes
Formation: Sitting in a circle.
Space: Can be played in a small space.

How to play

Sitting in a circle, the leader thinks of a phrase and whispers it to the person on their left.

That person must whisper the phrase into the ear of the person on their left. The message goes around the circle back to the beginning. Players can ask for the message to be repeated once only. The last player repeats the message aloud to see if it has changed. The outcome might be completely different to the original message. This is a great game to demonstrate how people re-interpret the messages that they hear. Try to get the players to think of phrases that are unusual or are verbally tricky.

21. Simon says

Age range: 5–6
Players: 5 or more
Set up time: under a minute
Playing time: 5–10 minutes
Formation: Anywhere in the space.
Space: Big enough for all players to move about in.

How to play

This is an easy game that helps players focus on a single task as a group. The aim of the game is to follow the instructions and stay in the game as long as possible.

The leader may begin as Simon. Everyone in the group must do what Simon says as long as Simon begins his instructions with 'Simon Says'. If he gives an instruction and demonstrates an action without beginning with 'Simon Says', players should ignore his command.

48

For example, if Simon says 'Simon Says put your hands on your hips' — then all players must put their hands on their hips. If he says, 'turn around' any player who turns around is out.

Simon may simply perform an action without speaking and any player who follows him is also out. The faster Simon gives his commands the more confused the players get.

The last player to stay in is the winner and becomes Simon in the next round.

22. Egg and spoon race

Age range: 5-6
Players: 3 or more
Set up time: 10 minutes
Playing time: 5–7 minutes
Formation: Ask the children to line up at the starting line for a race.
Space: Anywhere large.
Materials: Dessert spoons, raw eggs. You need one of each for each player. Using raw eggs makes it the most fun but only do so where appropriate. Alternatively hard boil the eggs.

How to play

Create a start and finish line. Line your players up with a spoon in their hand. Place an egg on each spoon. At the words 'Ready Set Go!' the players run with their eggs balancing on their spoon to the finish line. (You may want them to run back again to extend the race.) The first one to finish without dropping their egg wins.

Variations

Use teaspoons to make the race more difficult.
Ask the players to carry the spoon in their left hand.

50

23. Hide and seek

Age range: 5–6
Players: 5 or more
Set up time: Under a minute
Playing time: 10–20 minutes
Space: Inside or outside. Set up an area that is 'home base'.

How to play

One player is chosen to be in. He or she stands at 'home base' with their eyes closed and counts aloud to 30 seconds. The other players go and hide. On reaching 30 seconds, the player who is in calls out 'coming, ready or not'. They open their eyes and go to find where the players are hidden. The last player to be found wins.

To make the game more active, you can combine it with a game of 'tip'. Once the player who is in finds the hidden players they must run back to home base before the finder tips them. If they make it back they are safe. If they get tipped then they are in next.

24. Heads down, thumbs up!

Age range: 5–6 years
Players: 10 or more
Set up time: 1 minute
Playing time: 5–10 minutes
Formation: Seated in a group or at tables.
Space: Can be played in a small space.

How to play

This game is a good game to restore quiet to a rowdy group. Have the group seated on the floor or at tables. Select half the group to stand up and come to the front of the room or playing space. The rest of the children put their heads down with their eyes closed and thumbs sticking up.

52

The players at the front must sneak around and gently squeeze one person each on the thumb and then return to the front. Everyone is then told to open their eyes and the children who were touched each have a go at guessing which child touched them. If they get it right the children swap places, if not the children have another go. Repeat again by swapping the different groups of children.

Note

To make this game easier, select three players to be in. They squeeze the thumbs of one player each, who then try to guess who it was. Rotate players who are in.

25. Hopscotch

Age range: 5–6
Players: 2 or more
Set up time: 2 minutes
Playing time: 5–30 minutes
Space: To be played on concrete or a pavement.
Materials: A piece of chalk, a stone/marker for each player.

How to play

To set up, draw the hopscotch game on the ground with a piece of chalk. Make the squares big enough to hop on with one foot, around 30 cm by 30 cm.

The first player tosses their stone/marker into the first square. It must land fully within the square. If it touches a line or bounces out the player misses their turn. Once the stone lands in the first square, the player then hops through the course, hopping over the square with the marker in it.

Single squares must be hopped on with one foot. For the first single square, either foot may be used. Side by side squares are straddled, with the left foot landing in the left square, and the right foot landing in the right square. The top section with the half moon (number 10) is home and is considered a safe zone where you can stand with two feet. The player hops to 10 and back again.

If while hopping through the course in either direction the player steps on a line, misses a square, or loses balance, their turn ends.

Once the player successfully hops through the course then it is the next player's turn. The next player throws their stone into a square and hops through the course. On their next go, the first player picks up their stone from the first square and throws it into the second square. The second player's stone will still be on square one so the first player will need to hop straight over square 1 and 2 into square 3 to complete the course.

Players begin their turns where they last left off. The first player to complete a course for every numbered square on the court wins the game.

55

26. Apple bobbing

Age range: 5–6 and people of all ages.
Players: 3 or more
Set up time: 10–15 minutes
Playing time: 5–30 minutes depending on number of players.
Space: Outdoors or in a large hall.
Materials: Large tub or basin, water, apples, towels for drying wet faces.

How to play

This game is best played in summer. Fill a tub with water and then fill it with apples. Because apples are less dense than water, they will float on the surface. One by one, players try to catch an apple with their teeth. Use of hands is not allowed and players must hold their hands behind their backs. The apples will bob around as the players each try to catch one with their mouths only. Give each player the same time, say around 2 minutes, before moving to the next player's turn. They will end up with wet face and hair. Have a clean towel ready for drying faces and hair.

27. Treasure hunt

Age range: 5–6 (or children of varying ages working together)
Players: 5 or more
Set up time: 10–25 minutes
Playing time: As long as it takes until all of the treasure is found.
Space: A large space, either indoor or outdoor.
Materials: Chocolates, Easter eggs, anything yummy that is wrapped. If playing for a party, hide treasure that is all the same such as rocks spray-painted gold or something in theme with the party. The children can then find as much treasure as they like and bring it back to the adults to receive one present each.

How to play

Before the children arrive, hide the treasure. Place them where they can reach. When you say go, the children move off to find the treasure. The game ends when all the treasure is found.

Variation

Hot or cold
Say hot or cold depending on how close they are to the treasure. Hot indicates that they are close to the treasure and cold means they are further away.

Games for
7–9 year olds

28. Name and action

Age range: 7–9
Players: 5 or more
Set up time: 1 minute
Playing time: 2–5 minutes
Formation: Standing in a circle.
Space: Can be played in a small space.

How to play

This game helps players remember names by linking an action to each name and is a great warm-up game. Players stand in a circle. The leader starts by saying his or her name while performing a physical action at the same time. Together the group repeats the leader's name with the action. Play moves to the person on the right. The next person says their name and performs an action. The group repeats that person's name and their chosen action. Play continues until everyone has had a go. Watch each person perform their action and ask the group to try to do it in exactly the same way.

Example

The leader says his name, 'Thomas', and performs a karate kick at the same time. The group repeats his name and does the karate kick. The next person says her name, 'Rebecca', and turns around on the spot. The group repeats Rebecca's name while all turning around on the spot.

29. Name throw

Age range: 7–9
Players: 5 or more
Set up time: Under a minute
Playing time: 2–5 minutes
Formation: Standing in a circle.
Space: Can be played in a small space.
Materials: A ball.

How to play

Step 1

This is a great game for learning names. The leader starts with the ball. The objective is to throw the ball around the circle without dropping it and to learn people's names. The leader calls out their name and throws the ball to someone else in the circle. The person who catches the ball calls out their name and passes it to someone else. Continue until all names have been heard once or twice. If you want to make it easier ask everyone to start with their hands out in front of them. Once they have caught and thrown the ball they can put them down at their side.

Step 2

The person with the ball then calls out someone else's name in the circle and throws the ball to them. The player who catches the ball calls out someone's name and throws the ball to that person. Continue until everyone in the circle has received and thrown the ball once.

Step 3

See the game 'Name jump' for 10–12 year olds for the third step of the Ball Name game on p. 62.

Variation

For the littlies

Little kids (5–6 year olds) can also play this game by sitting in a circle and rolling the ball to each other.

30. Giant letters

Age range: 7–9
Players: 8 or more
Set up time: Under a minute
Playing time: 5–7 minutes
Formation: Random.
Space: Indoors or outdoors and can be played in a small space.

How to play

The aim of the game is for the group to physically create the letters of the alphabet without speaking. The leader calls out, 'Make the letter K'. The group works together to make a representation of the letter K (they may decide to stand or lie down feet to head creating the shape of 'K'). Remind them not to speak. The leader continues to call out letters of the alphabet. The group will become quicker with practice. For more of a challenge, ask them to make two letter words.

Variation

Knife and Fork on p.136 is a good game to play immediately after this one depending on how keen and cooperative your group is.

31. Untie the knot

Age range: 7–9
Players: 8 or more
Set up time: Under a minute
Playing time: 3–7 minutes
Formation: A huddle or tight circle.
Space: Can be played in a small space depending on the size of the group.

How to play

The aim of the game is to finish in a circle holding hands. Players stand in a tight circle and randomly take hold of other players' hands. The puzzle is for the group to untangle themselves without letting go of each other's hands, to finish in a large circle. They will need to step over or go under other players' joined hands and depending on the size of the group they may end up with a few smaller circles. Some players may end up facing opposite directions when they finish in the circle. This is OK.

32. Silent cow

Age range: 7–9
Players: 8 or more
Set up time: Under a minute
Playing time: 3–5 minutes
Formation: Random crawling on hands and knees with eyes closed. Define boundaries
Space: Can be played in a room with enough space for all the players to crawl about.

How to play

All players start on their hands and knees in the playing area imagining they are cows in a field. It is best to play this game on carpet or mats. The leader asks all players to close their eyes. The leader moves around the players and quietly tips one player on the head. That player becomes the silent cow. All the cows crawl around the space on their hands and knees with their eyes closed. If they bump into or touch another 'cow' they 'moo' in greeting and the other cow 'moos' back. If a 'cow' bumps into the silent cow, the silent cow does not moo back so they know that they have bumped into the silent cow. If a player bumps into the silent cow then they must both stop where they are and freeze. That 'cow' becomes a silent cow as well and stays put. Any 'cow' who bumps into the silent cows becomes a silent cow and freezes. The game ends when all cows have frozen as silent cows.

33. Clap clap, click click

Age range: 7–9
Players: 5 or more
Set up time: Under a minute
Playing time: 2–5 minutes
Formation: Sitting or standing in a circle.
Space: Can be played in a small space.

How to play

This is a great game for learning names. The leader demonstrates the rhythm. The rhythm is two claps of the hand and a click of the fingers on the right hand and then a click of the fingers on the left hand. It sounds like clap clap click click. Practice the rhythm with the group first.

Begin the clap clap click click rhythm. Keep the rhythm going at all times. The leader starts by calling out his or her name on the click click of the fingers. Keeping with the rhythm, everyone in the circle repeats the leader's name on the next click click of the fingers without missing a beat. The person to the left then calls out their name on the next click click of the fingers and the group repeats it in unison on the next click click. Continue around the circle until everyone has called out their name and it has been repeated by everyone in the circle.

Remembering names

Begin the clap clap click click rhythm. The leader starts by saying his or her name on the click click of the fingers and then saying another person's name on the second go. The person whose name is called then takes up the lead and calls out another person's name. The key is to stay with the rhythm of clap clap click click and call out a person's name on the click of the fingers. When your name is called out it is your turn to call out another person's name on the next click of the fingers.

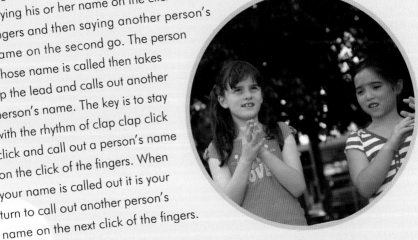

Examples

If the leader's name is Belinda and she chooses to call Joshua. After two claps Belinda says her name on the click of the fingers.

On the next round she calls out Joshua's name on the click of the fingers.

Joshua then calls out another person's name on the next click of the fingers and that person calls out someone else's name after the next two claps.

34. Captain's coming

Age range: 7–9
Players: 8 or more
Set up time: 2 minutes
Playing time: 5–15 minutes
Formation: Players stand together in the space.
Space: The game can be adapted to the size of the space you are in.

How to play

Players stand in the centre of the room imagining they are sailors on a boat. Before you start the game, explain the commands to the group and show them the corresponding actions. Practise a few times for a warm-up to the actual game. The supervisor can be the 'captain' or a 'captain' is chosen and calls out the commands. The players must perform the actions as quickly as they can. They must continue to perform these actions until the next command is called out. If a player is not quick enough, does the wrong action or fails to find a group the captain eliminates them. The commands can be mixed up and called out more than once.

When the leader calls out 'Captain's coming', all the players stand to attention making a salute with their right hand. They must not move or perform another command until the leader calls out 'Captain's going'. In the same way as in the game Simon Says on p.50, if the leader calls out another command before calling 'Captain's going', such as 'Scrub the deck', any player who gets down on their hands and knees to scrub the deck is out. The leader must always call 'Captain's going' after 'Captain's coming' for the players to be allowed to perform other commands.

The commands and actions are as follows:

Captain's coming – all stand at attention with a salute.

Captain's going – Players put their thumb to their nose and waggle their fingers.

To the ship – Everyone runs to the right (starboard).

To the shore – Everyone runs to the left (port).

Scrub the deck – Everyone on hands and knees pretend to scrub the floor.

Climb the ropes – While standing, everyone pretends to climb up ropes.

Man overboard – Players lie on their backs and kicks their legs in the air.

Row the lifeboats – Find a partner, sit together and row

Hit the deck – Fall to the floor and lie on your stomach.

Submarines – Lie on your back and stick one leg straight up (for the periscope).

Crow's nest – Two players stand back to back and link arms at the elbows.

Captain's girlfriend – Players thrust out their hip and pretend to swing a sash with their hand and call out woo-woo! (This is optional but kids generally love this.)

Choose as many or as few of these commands as you like depending on the group and the amount of time you have.

35. Teepees and Indians

Age range: 7–9
Players: 10 or more. Even numbers required.
Set up time: Under a minute
Playing time: 5–10 minutes
Formation: Sitting and standing in a circle.
Space: Enough room for players to run around the outside of the group sitting in a circle.

How to play

Players pair up. This game is played in a circle. One is the Indian and sits on the ground, cross-legged. The other is the Teepee and stands behind their (Indian) partner with their legs apart and arms above their heads with palms touching (so they look like a Teepee). Indicate the direction they run. Also instruct faster players to run around the outside of the slower ones.

When you call out 'Indians'. The Indians (who are sitting cross-legged in front of their teepees), crawl between their Teepee's legs, run around the circle and back to their spot. The first one back is the winner of that go.

When you call 'Teepees', the Teepees have to run around their Indians (clockwise) then run around the circle and back to their spot.

To play, randomly call out Indians or Teepees. The children must then anticipate when it will be their turn to go. The aim is for the player to get back to their spot the quickest. Swap around.

Variation

Place a ball (any object works) in the centre of the circle. The fastest player must pick up the ball from the centre of the circle before sitting down. They return it to the centre before the next go. Alert the kids to not bump heads when racing for the ball.

73

36. The Simpsons

Players: 10 or more
Set up time: 1–2 minutes
Playing time: 5–15 minutes
Formation: Scattered running
Space: A large area of 10 by 10 metres. Divide the playing area into two 'safe' zones about 10 metres apart.

How to play

The group decides on three characters from the TV show, The Simpsons, such as Bart, Marge and Lisa. Each player decides in their head which character they want to be. One person is chosen to be 'in'. The players stand on one side and the person who is in stands in the centre of the space.

The person in the middle calls one of the three Simpson character's names, such as Bart. All players who are Bart must run to the other side without being tipped by the player who is in. If tipped, a player must sit down where they are. Play continues in the same way for the other characters. Once all players are on the other side they run back when their character's name is called.

If the person in the middle calls out 'The Simpsons' everyone must run. The players sitting on the ground may then reach out and tip the legs of the other players. Again any players that are tipped must sit down where they are. Continue to play until everyone is out and sitting down, except the person who is in.

37. Cat and mouse

Age range: 7–9
Players: 8 or more
Set up time: Under a minute
Playing time: 5–7 minutes
Formation: Scattered running
Space: An area of 10 by 10 metres. Clearly identify the area of play by using markings, or simple instructions.

How to play

Children form pairs and stand randomly in the space with their arms linked and both hands on their hips. Choose two people to be in and this pair separates – one is the cat (the chaser) and the other is the mouse.

The cat begins to chase the mouse. To avoid being tipped, the mouse must link arms with a pair and the person on the opposite end must unlink their arms. That person becomes the new mouse. The cat chases the new mouse. If the mouse gets tipped, they change roles.

The mouse can link arms with any player in the space as often as needed and there is no limit to how many times a player becomes a cat or mouse. If playing this game for the first time, call out change when a cat tips a mouse so they know to swap roles and continue the game. It is a fast game.

38. Red light, green light with variations

Age range: 7–9

Players: 10 or more

Set up time: Under a minute

Playing time: 5–10 minutes

Formation: This game involves the group running forward in a line.

Space: Needs a large open space to accommodate the children running.

How to play

This is a physical game that involves running, sneaking and freezing. Play the game as explained for the 5–6 year old game on p. 30 once or twice to warm-up the group. Then play the game with the following variations. The player who is in does not call out red or green light, they just turn around.

Variation

Facial expressions
Give the players an emotion such as 'surprised'. When the person at the front turns around they must freeze with the look of surprise on their face.

Variation

Piggy-back

Match smaller players with bigger players. The big kids have to piggy-back the smaller kids and then play the game. If one player moves then both go back to the start. If the game is long and the kids begin to tire, they can link arms instead. Ask the kids to walk fast not run when carrying another player on their back.

Variation

Passing something

As well as moving forward, the players have to pass an item between them (such as a ball) behind their backs. They must still freeze when the traffic light turns around and the item must remain hidden. The item must not stay in any one person's hand for longer than 20 seconds. The traffic light must guess who is holding the item. If they get it right they win and the person caught holding the item is in next. Or if they don't guess correctly the first person to tap the traffic light on the back wins.

77

39. Rock, paper, scissors

Age range: 7–9
Players: 15 or more
Set up time: 1–2 mintues
Playing time: 5–10 minutes
Formation: Create two 'safe' zones 5 to 10 paces apart.
Space: A large room, hall or outside on the grass.

How to play

This game is a group game of 'Rock, Paper, Scissors'. Two people stand facing one another with their hands held in a fist at elbow height. Together they count 1, 2, 3 or say 'rock, paper, scissors' aloud. As they do this they raise one hand in a fist and swing it down on each word. On the third count each player 'throws' their hand gesture. The player with the winning hand gesture wins.

* Rock beats (blunts) scissors.
* Paper beats (wraps) rock.
* Scissors beats (cuts) paper.

Hand gestures
Rock = Clenched fist.
Paper = Flat horizontal hand.
Scissors = Make a pair of scissors.
with your fingers.

How to play as a group making the signs with your body

Teach the players the moves described on the following page using the whole body to indicate paper, rock or scissors. Divide the group in half to create two teams. The teams stand about 5 paces apart in their safe zones. Ask the two teams to quickly and secretly decide on what sign they will choose to do. Members of a team all choose and perform the same sign. Once they have decided, the two teams walk towards each other into the middle of the space. They stand in a line facing each about a foot apart.

Together they count 1, 2, 3 and then all perform their action of either paper, rock or scissors. Members of the team who perform the winning action must then chase and tip as many players on the opposite team before they can

continued overleaf

run back to their safety zone. Players that are tipped join the winning team and the teams re-group to play again. Play many times and watch the two teams change in size.

The game ends when there is no second team left (that is, all players have been tipped and joined one team). This does not always happen so finish the game when you feel it is appropriate.

Variation

Body positions
Rock = Arms crossed on chest with fists clenched.
Paper = Arms straight up above head with flat palms.
Scissors = Move forearms up and down with bent elbows like a robotic scissor action.

40. Dead ant

Age range: 7–9
Players: 8 or more
Set up time: Under a minute
Playing time: 5–10 minutes
Formation: Scattered running.
Space: An area about 10 by 10 metres with play boundaries marked out.
Materials: 4 hoops or square mats.

How to play

Place 4 hoops (or square mats) randomly on the floor. The hoops represent the hospital. Select one player to be in – they will chase the others. When they tip someone, that person must lay down on their back on the floor with both arms and legs sticking up, just like a dead ant. Other players rescue the dead ant by carrying them by their arms and legs to the hospital. Once the dead ant reaches the hospital, they become alive again. Ants cannot be tipped while they are in hospital but can only stay there for less than 10 seconds. Ants carrying the dead ant to the hospital are safe until they deliver them. If you have a large group of children, select a few of them to be in.

Before the game demonstrate how to lift a dead ant safely. Four players must take either an arm or a leg each. The dead ant must stay rigid while they are being carried. If you are playing with larger children, two players can take either an arm and a leg or two arms or two legs each and carry the ant.

41. Secret leader

Age range: 7–9
Players: 5 or more
Set up time: Under a minute
Playing time: 5–6 minutes (depending on size of group)
Formation: Sitting or standing in a circle facing inwards.

How to play

Everyone sits or stands in a circle. One player leaves the room. This person becomes the 'guesser'. Select a player who will be the secret leader. The leader begins an action such as snapping fingers, patting the tummy or slapping knees, and everyone in the circle follows the leader.

The guesser returns to the room and joins in the circle. The guesser must try to figure out who the secret leader is. As the guesser looks around, the secret leader must change the action frequently without being detected. The guesser has three chances to guess correctly. If the guesser is correct that person becomes the new leader.

42. Hospital tip

Age range: 7–9
Players: 10 or more
Set up time: Under a minute
Playing time: 5 minutes
Formation: A game of tip – random running and chasing.
Space: In a large space of 10 by 10 metres

How to play

One player is chosen to be Mr/Ms Sick. Mr/Ms Sick chases all the other players. When a player is tipped they must cover their 'wound' (where they have been tipped) with one hand. When a player is tipped a second time, they must cover their wound with the other hand. The third time a player is tipped they are out. To speed up the game you can choose two or more players to be Mr/Ms Sick.

If a player removes their hand from their wound while running they are out.

43. Tie stomp

Age range: 7–9
Players: 8 or more
Set up time: 1 minute
Playing time: 5 minutes
Space: A large space 10 by 10 metres.
Materials: One man's tie for every player.

How to play

Everyone tucks a tie into the back of their pants so that it touches the ground. Players run around and stomp on the ties trailing behind each player. If you lose a tie you are out. Ties that are stomped on are collected by the supervisor of the game or left on the floor.

The winner is the last person who is left in the game with a tie.

44. Egg or ball toss

Age range: 7–9
Players: 6 or more
Set up time: 1 minute
Playing time: 1–2 minutes
Space: Indoors or outdoors in a large area.
Materials: One raw or hard-boiled egg or a ball for each pair of children.

How to play

The children form pairs and then stand about 30 cm away from the other partner. Begin by tossing the egg to your partner. After every throw one person takes a step back. Continue to play until you drop your egg. The pair who is the furthest apart wins. This game can also work with a small ball for each pair. The pair to get the furthest apart from one another without dropping their ball wins.

45. The hand game

Age range: 7–9
Players: 6 or more
Set up time: 1–3 minutes
Playing time: 2–5 minutes
Formation: A circle with children lying on their stomachs facing into the middle of the circle.
Space: This game can be played in small space.

How to play

Ask the children lying on their stomachs, with their arms bent at the elbow and palms flat on the ground. Another variation is to kneel on all fours with shoulders almost touching.

Everyone places their hands directly in front of them on the ground so there is a circle of hands. Players create an alternating hand pattern by placing their hand between the hands of the person either side of them. This means there are two people's hands placed between a player's left and right hand.

Looking down onto the group the hands would look like this: (From left to right) My LEFT hand, then the person on my left's RIGHT hand, then the person on my right's LEFT hand, then my RIGHT hand, and so on.

The leader decides on the tapping direction and slaps their hand on the ground once. The hand next to theirs then slaps the surface, then the next hand and so on. Each person slaps his or her hand once only and the next hand must follow.

A double slap changes direction. Anyone can do a double slap of the hand at any stage in the game.

Variation

Optional Elimination
If someone slaps out of turn then they are out. They remove their hands from the circle. The game is over when there are only two people left.

Variation

It can also be played around a table. Either way, everyone must have his or her hands ready to slap a flat surface.

46. Murder wink

Age range: 7–9
Players: 8 or more
Set up time: Under a minute
Playing time: 5–10 minutes
Formation: Sitting in a circle facing inwards.
Space: This game can be played in a small space.

How to play

Players sit in a circle facing each other. One person is chosen to be the detective and they leave the room. The rest of the group close their eyes and the leader taps someone on the head. That person is the murderer. Everyone opens their eyes and the detective is invited back into the room and sits in the middle of the circle.

The murderer 'kills' people by winking at them without letting the detective see. The detective's job is to work out who the murderer is. Players look around the circle and make eye contact. If a player is winked at, he or she must die as dramatically as possible. They then stay lying down or sit outside of the circle.

The detective has 3 chances to guess who the murderer is. Play this a number of times.

47. Musical chairs

Age range: 7–9
Players: 10 or more
Set up time: 2–5 minutes
Playing time: 5–10 minutes
Formation: Chairs placed in a row back to back forming a line. There needs to be one chair fewer than the number of players.
Space: In a space large enough for the chairs and for people to run around the outside of them.

How to play

The children need to circle the line of chairs. Indicate the direction they will be moving around them. When the music starts players must walk around the chairs. When the music stops players quickly sit on the nearest chair. The player who misses out on a seat is out. All players then stand and one chair is removed. Repeat and keep going until there are only two people remaining and one chair. The person to sit in the last chair wins.

Variation

Give commands before you start the music each time. You can ask them to skip, walk with their hands on their hips, walk on tippy-toes or do the train (holding on the the hips of the person in front).

48. The Ha

Age range: 7–9
Players: 10 or more
Set up time: 1–2 minutes
Playing time: 1–2 minutes
Formation: Standing in a circle facing inwards.
Space: This game can be played in a small space.

This is a great favourite of mine, which I regularly use to finish a session. It is a clear indication for the children that the session has come to an end and they like to make the loud 'Ha' noise to finish with. Kids love it.

The leader needs to take some time to demonstrate what 'The Ha' is before getting started.

The Ha begins from a neutral standing position. Jump your legs apart. At the same time, bring your arms up so they cross your body with bent elbows at shoulder height, fists clenched. At the same time, make a deep loud 'Ha' sound landing with your knees bent. It looks like a move from the Maori Haka dance. Practise it alltogether in the group.

How to play

Part 1: All players stand in a circle with their arms by their side. The leader, who is also standing in the circle, will be the one to initiate the Ha! The leader waits for the group to be ready and the

others wait for their lead. When the leader initiates the Ha! the rest of the players must follow as quickly as possible.

Part 2: Once in this position, the players are asked to close their eyes. The leader walks around the outside of the circle and taps one player on the head. When the leader gets back to his position, players are asked to open their eyes. The leader asks all the players to look at an imaginary spot in the middle of the circle. While doing this, ask the players to use their peripheral vision to also focus on the rest of the group.

The player who was tapped on the head will lead the Ha! They will go, only when he or she thinks the group is focused and ready. If children are fidgeting they wait until everyone is ready. The group

continued overleaf

does not know who it will be so they wait in anticipation all focusing on the centre of the circle but remaining aware of all players in the circle. When the group is focused the player who was tapped on the head initiates the Ha! Everyone follows. It looks like the whole group did the Ha! spontaneously.

Variation

For 10–12 year olds
Play part one and two first. All players stand in a circle with their hands at their sides, focusing on a point in the centre of the circle and using their peripheral vision to be aware of all the other players. The leader explains that any one player can choose to initiate the Ha! at any time they think the group is ready. When a player initiates the Ha! all players must join in and do the Ha!

49. Mirror

Age range: 7–9
Players: 6 or more
Set up time: 1–2 minutes.
Playing time: 5–6 minutes
Formation: Pairs standing in a line facing one another.
Space: This game can be played in a small space.

How to play

This game is played in complete silence. Get the players to pair up. The partners in each pair stand 30 cm apart. Decide who will lead and who will follow. The leader starts with their hands up at shoulder height and palms facing out. They move their hands and their partner mirrors their movements.

As the players become more at ease they may become more experimental with their movements. They may play with different heights. Swap around after a few minutes.

Variation

In unison
Each pair stands about 30 cm apart, facing each other. The leader calls out 'in unison'. This means the pairs work together creating the movement and there is no dedicated leader or follower. The pairs simply switch between the roles fluidly to the point whereby they may feel like they are working in unison.

50. Who am I?

Age range: 7–9
Players: 5 or more. Can be played in pairs
Set up time: 5–6 minutes
Playing time: 5–20 minutes
Space: Indoors or in a small space.
Materials: Post-it notes, pen

How to play

Everyone sits in a circle. Give everyone a pen and post-it note and ask the players to secretly write down the name of a famous person. They then stick the post-it note on the forehead of the person to their right without that person seeing what is written on it. If children get stuck thinking up names the leader can help individuals or secretly write up all the names of famous people to start the game. Pick people that they relate to or have discussed in class or in the group.

Players must find out the identity of their famous person by asking the whole group Yes or No questions about who they are. Their team-mates can answer only with 'yes' or 'no'. Each player gets three questions then move on.

Example questions are:
    Am I a man?
    Am I a musician/writer/inventor etc?
    Do I live in Australia?

The first person to guess correctly is the winner. The winner stays in the game to help answer questions of the other players. Play continues until everyone has guessed correctly. If you have a large group make smaller groups of four or five players or do the exercise in pairs.

Variation

In the car
This game can be played in the car. One person is in and they think of a famous person. The others have to ask Yes or No questions to find out who it is that they are thinking of. The person who guesses the right answer wins and they are in next.

51. Memory

Age range: 7–9
Players: 2 or more
Set up time: 5–10 minutes
Playing time: 5–20 minutes
Formation: Sitting in a circle at a table.
Space: This game can be played in a small space.
Materials: 45–60 random objects, a large piece of cloth, pens, paper.

How to play

This game is great for developing memory skills. Gather 15–20 random objects from around the house. Choose a couple of items that 'match' with each other such as a bowl and spoon or a comb and brush. Players leave the room while you place the objects in the centre or on the table. Cover the objects with a cloth. Invite the players back, sit them down and allow them to view the group of objects for two minutes.

After two minutes, remove the objects and ask the players to write down as many objects that they can remember on a piece of paper. Compare the results and discuss the ways they used to remember the objects.

96

Association by silly images

Have 15–20 new objects. Before you show the objects to the group ask them to remember (visualise) each object in a funny location in their own house. As a suggestion, 'you may imagine a set of keys swimming in the bathtub'. The sillier the image, the easier it is to remember. Allow the players to view the objects for two minutes then remove them. Ask them to write down what they can remember. Compare results with the first exercise.

Make up a story

Have 15–20 new objects. Before you show the objects, ask the players to make up a story in their heads using all the objects they are about to see. Allow them to view the objects for 2 minutes. Remove the objects and ask the players to write down what they recalled. Compare results and you may also like to compare stories. The sillier the story the easier it is to remember.

You should find that players remember more items using association than when they did the exercise the first time. Remember that players are only allowed to write once they objects are covered up or removed from view and not before.

97

52. Sack race

Age range: 7–9
Players: 3 or more
Set up time: 10 minutes
Playing time: 5–10 minutes.
Formation: Jumping forward in a line.
Space: Outdoors or in a large hall with space to run a race.
Materials: A large hessian sack or an old tough pillow case for each player.
A whistle (optional).

How to play

Create a start and finish line about 10 metres apart. Lay the sacks out on the ground about 2–3 metres from the start line. Alternatively they can start standing in their sacks.

Players line up at the start line. On the word go, players run to a sack, put both feet in and jumping towards the finish line. Players must keep both feet in the sack and can only jump. They should have one hand on the sack at all times and must keep it around their waist. The first player to reach the finish line wins.

Variation

Relay

Play the sack race as a relay. You will need at least 8 players for this version, but only two sacks.

Split players up into even numbered teams. Half of the players will line up at the start line and the other half at the finish line (that is, a team of 4 has two players on either side facing each other). If you have one team with an odd number of players they can choose a player to run twice, once at the start and then again at the end.

The first player for each of the teams will line up at the start line with both feet in the sack. On the word 'go' (or whistle) they must jump to the other side and give their sack to their team member. The next player climbs into the empty sack and jumps back. Repeat this sequence until the entire team has switched sides. The first team to get all members to the opposite sides without breaking the rules wins.

Variation

Longer course

Split the players into even numbered teams. Line the teams up on the starting line with the team members standing behind each other and the first player of each team standing in a sack. Place a marker/cone about 10 metres away from the start line.

On the word 'go', or at the whistle the first players in each team jumps to the marker, goes around it and jumps back to the start. They give the sack to the next player who repeats the task. The first team to successfully get all players around the cone and sit down in a line wins.

53. Three-legged race

Age range: 7–9
Players: 6 or more
Set up time: 10–15 minutes
Playing time: 5–15 minutes.
Formation: Players team up in pairs, lining up in a row.
Space: Outdoors or in a large hall with a start and finish line marked on the ground, approximately 10 metres apart.
Materials: An old stocking or tie for each pair.

How to play

Ask the pair to stand side by side so that their legs closest together are almost touching. Tie an old stocking around the legs of the two players. Give the pairs a little moment to practise walking and running together so they can get a feel of the rhythm.

To start the race, pairs line up at the start line with their arms around each other's waist for support. On the word go or at the whistle the pairs run to the finish line with their legs tied. The first pair to get to the finish line wins.

You can create a three legged relay or obstacle race depending on the size and energy of the group.

Make sure you play this game on a soft surface, such as grass or mats, as the pairs will inevitably fall down.

54. Sardines

Age range: 7–9
Players: 3 or more
Set up time: 1–2 minutes
Playing time: 10–20 minutes
Formation: Scattered hiding and seeking in a large area.
Space: It's easier inside or where there are good large hiding places.

How to play

Sardines is a variation of Hide and Seek. A player is chosen to be 'in'. Instead of searching for team-mates, the player who is in must hide. The rest of the players stand together, close their eyes and count to 30 while the person hides. When they reach 30 seconds, they open their eyes and go in search of the hidden player. When a player finds the child who is hiding, they quietly hide with them. As more children find the hidden player they must all squash in together until the last player finds the group. It gets very squashy as more players discover the hiding spot and sneak in to hide from the others. The last person to find the group hiding together is in next.

55. Spin the bottle in reverse

Age range: 7–9 (or children of various ages)
Players: 5 or more
Set up time: 10 minutes
Playing time: 10–20 minutes
Formation: Sitting in a circle, facing inwards.
Space: This game can be played inside.
Materials: Dressing-up clothes (choose bright, silly clothes), hats, wigs, ties, necklaces and a bottle.

How to play

The leader places a bottle on its side in the middle of the circle. Have a basket of clothes outside the circle. A player stands up and spins the bottle, then sits down. When the bottle comes to rest with the neck of the bottle pointing to a player, that player must get up and put something on from the dressing-up basket. The rest of the group counts to 10 while the person tries to put on an item of clothing. If they have an item of clothing only half on when the counting reaches 10 seconds, they are not

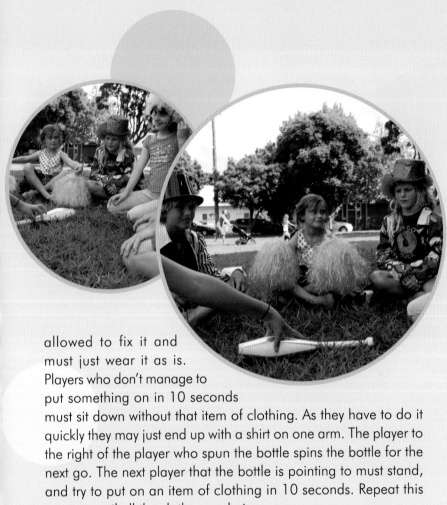

allowed to fix it and
must just wear it as is.
Players who don't manage to
put something on in 10 seconds
must sit down without that item of clothing. As they have to do it
quickly they may just end up with a shirt on one arm. The player to
the right of the player who spun the bottle spins the bottle for the
next go. The next player that the bottle is pointing to must stand,
and try to put on an item of clothing in 10 seconds. Repeat this
process until all the clothes are being worn.

The player wearing the most items of clothes wins. (The hats,
wigs and sunglasses will be chosen first. The more difficult items of
clothes like tops, dresses and overalls will be left till last.)

If 10 seconds is too easy for the group reduce the time to less
so that it becomes more of a challenge. If it is too quick for the
group give them a little longer.

56. Photographic treasure hunt

Age range: 7–9 (or children of varying ages working together)
Players: 3 or more
Set up time: 30 minutes–90 minutes
Formation: Children work in a group searching for clues and hiding spots.
Space: Indoors or outdoors.
Materials: Digital camera, printer, photographic paper, scissors, envelope and the treasure. If you don't have the time or resources to do this, cut-out pictures from magazines to represent different places/rooms in the house. Or if you can, draw the pictures yourself. A 'treasure' to hide.

To set up

Walk around the house taking close-up digital photos of places or things in the house, such as window-sills, the bottom of bookcases, inside cupboards, picture frames and lamps. Remember that these places are where you will be hiding clues so look for nooks and crannies to hide things in. Select the 10 best pictures and print them out. Hide the treasure and keep the photo that leads to the treasure to the side. Chose one photo to be the first clue, cut it into a number of pieces and place it in an envelope. Now hide the rest of the photos in sequence so that each clue leads to the hiding place of the next clue and finally the treasure. Finish with the last clue that you kept aside that leads to the treasure. Keep a list of where each photo is hidden and number it, just in case a clue goes missing.

How to play

Give the children the photo in pieces in an envelope. The children put the puzzle of the picture together and use the image to work out where it is in the house or garden. They will go looking for that place and there you will have hidden the next clue, which they will find and it will lead to the next clue and so on. The final clue leads to the treasure.

You can play photographic treasure hunt with children 5–6 years old by using easily identifiable pictures to lead to the next clue. You can also play it with older children 10–12 years of age but you will need to make the images very obscure so that it becomes a real challenge for the children to solve each clue.

Games for
10–12 year olds

57. Name jump

Age range: 10–12
Players: 6 or more
Set up time: 1–2 minutes
Playing time: 2–5 minutes
Formation: Standing in a circle, facing inwards.
Space: This game can be played in a small space.
Materials: A ball.

How to play

Standing in a circle play a few rounds of Name Throw as described in the introduction games for 7–9 year olds on p. 62 then lead into this variation.

The player with the ball calls out the name of another player but passes the ball to someone else. The person who catches the ball must throw the ball to the person whose name was called by the player who passed them the ball, but while they throw the ball, they call out another person's name. The person who catches the ball must pass the ball to the name the thrower called and call out a new person's name.

58. Line ups

Age range: 10–12
Players: 3 or more
Set up time: Under a minute
Playing time: 2–5minutes
Space: Indoors in a small space.

How to play

Give the group a number of instructions that they must carry out without speaking. Create as many categories as you like. This game is played in silence so remind the group not to talk.

Examples

* Line up from the smallest to the tallest.
* Line up from the darkest eye colour to the lightest.
* Line up from the longest hair to the shortest hair.
* Get into a line of the month of your birth.
* Get into groups of star signs.
* Get into groups according to how you traveled here today.
* Get into groups of how many people living in your house.

59. Scream

Age range: 10–12
Players: 10 or more
Set up time: Under a minute
Playing time: 2–5 minutes
Formation: Divide the group in two and have them stand in two circles close to each other.
Space: In a hall or outside.

How to play

Players stand in the circle looking down to the ground. When the leader calls out 'GO!' all the players must look up and stare into the eyes of only one person in the circle. If that person happens to be staring back at them, then both players scream 'ahhh' and run to join the other circle. Play again and again as the sizes of the circles continue to change.

60. Name and song

Age range: 10–12
Players: 6 or more
Set up time: Under a minute
Playing time: 2–3 minutes
Formation: Standing in a circle, facing inwards.
Space: This game can be played in a small space.

How to play

This is good to play with a group where everyone knows each other. One player says their name out loud and sings the refrain or line of any song they like. Everyone repeats the person's name and sings the phrase of the song in unison. The next person has a turn until everyone in the group has had a go.

Example

Thomas says his name 'Thomas' then sings; 'Old Macdonald had a farm'. The whole group says 'Thomas' and then sings 'Old Macdonald had a farm. Continue with the next player on the left of the first person who started.

61. Group juggle

Age range: 10–12
Players: 5 or more
Set up time: 1 minute
Playing time: 5–10 minutes
Formation: Standing in a circle.
Space: Big enough for all players to stand in a circle.
Materials: Enough balls for each person, or use a variety of soft, silly items such as a rubber chicken or a teddy bear.

How to play

All players stand in a circle with their hands out in front of them. The leader throws the ball to someone in the circle and calls out their name. The player who catches the ball then throws the ball to someone else in the circle, calling that player's name. Once a person has received the ball they put their hands behind their back so they are not thrown the ball again. Continue this process so that everyone has caught the ball once and thrown it to another player. Tell the players to remember who they threw the ball to. The last player to receive the ball must throw it back to the leader. They will always throw the ball to that same person and receive the ball from the same person.

The leader starts again and throws the ball to the person he threw it to the first time around. As the ball moves on, the leader adds new balls into the circle by throwing more balls to the person he threw to originally. Meanwhile the original ball is still going

Begin with a ball and then throw in a range of different objects, such as listed above in 'Materials'.

around. See how many balls the group can keep in the air at once. Once the first ball returns to the leader don't let it stop, keep the rotations going by throwing it on. If a player drops a ball they can try to pick it up but they should leave it if it causes them to miss the next ball.

Players should catch the ball with two hands and throw with one. They must always call the name of the person they throw the ball to (even though it is the same person every time).

62. Pirate raid

Age range: 10–12
Players: 4 or more
Set up time: 1 minute
Playing time: 5–10 minutes
Formation: One player (or four even groups of players) in the four corners of the playing space and a pile of treasure (balls) in the middle.
Space: An indoor or outdoor space of 10 by 10 metres.
Materials: 60 balls or other items, such as soft toys.
Create four stations with hoops or boxes for each corner of the room.
If you don't have hoops or boxes, use a piece of carpet or newspaper to indicate where players must place their balls.

How to play

Divide the group into four teams. Place a hoop or box, or draw a circle in chalk in the four corners of the playing field or space. These are islands. Place a pile of the balls (or other items) in the middle of the space. Make sure that the islands are equidistant from the centre island where all the balls are placed.

The four teams (or the four players) stand at their islands in the four corners of the space. The aim is to collect as much treasure from the island in the middle of the room and take it back to their island. When the leader says 'Go", players run and collect treasure from the middle island. They can only take one piece of treasure at a time. They run back to their island and place the treasure in their island before returning to the centre to get another piece. At any time, players can steal treasure from the islands of the other teams but only taking one piece at a time and taking it back to their island. Players continue this process until there is no more treasure left on the middle island, and then the leader calls out 'Stop!' The team with the most treasure on their island after the leader calls stop wins. To make it more interesting you can allocate a value to different items of treasure.

63. Zip, zap, zoom

Age range: 10–12
Players: 8 or more
Set up time: 1-3 minutes
Playing time: 5–10 minutes
Formation: Standing in a circle, facing inwards
Space: This game can be played in a small space.

How to play

This is a great game that creates group focus. It is quick and exciting. Make sure you take the time to explain the game and only play elimination once everyone is clear on the directions.

Players stand in a circle. The aim of the game is to keep the clap (energy) moving around the circle. Players pass the clap around the circle by placing their hands together (making a clap sound) and then moving their hands in the direction they want the clap to go. Players call out a command (see below) as they pass the clap.

Start by passing the 'Zip' clap around the circle. The leader begins by making a sharp 'Zip' sound and a fast clap, which they pass to the person on their right. They in turn pass it on to the next person on their right. It must go one at a time. Once the group has done a full rotation of 'Zip', introduce the 'Zap' clap into the circle. 'Zap' is a clap in the opposite direction – to the left. Practise the 'Zap' in the group.

Then introduce the 'Screech', which changes direction of the clap. A player passes a 'Zip' to the player to their right and they put their hands up and say 'screech'. Then the player who 'Zipped' must turn the other way and 'Zap' the person to their left. The 'Zap' continues around the circle until another player decides to say 'Screech' and it changes direction again. Practise this.

Introduce passing the clap across the circle with the 'Zoom'. After receiving a 'Zoom' a player may choose to 'Zip', 'Zap' or 'Zoom' someone else. You cannot 'Screech' a 'Zoom!' You can only 'Zoom' someone who is not directly on your right or left.

To play elimination, start the 'Zip' round the circle. Allow the players to 'Screech', 'Zap', 'Zip' and 'Zoom' one another. If a player makes a mistake such as says the wrong word, does not clap or does not respond quickly they are out. They must sit down for the rest of the game. Keep the energy moving quickly. As players become better at it, become tougher on the rules. When there are only three players left they play without 'Zoom'. The two players left become the winners. Play a few times. Remember – you can't 'Screech' a 'Zoom', must 'Zoom' across the circle and a fast game is a good game.

Commands

'Zip' signals to pass the clap to the right.
Call out 'Zip', clap hands together and move hands to the right.
'Zap' signals to pass the clap to the left.
Call out 'Zap', clap hands together and move hands to the left.
'Zoom' signals to pass the clap across the circle.
Call out 'Zoom', clap hands, and point to someone across the circle.
'Screech' signals to change direction.
Call out 'Screech' and hold both hands up in the air. This blocks the Zip or Zap and forces the player to change direction.

64. The chair game

Age range: 10–12
Players: 7 or more
Set up time: 2 minutes
Playing time: 5–15 minutes
Formation: Establish the play boundaries. Each player takes a chair and places it randomly within the play space.
Space: Played in a room large enough for chairs to be placed randomly and for players to run between the chairs.
Materials: One chair per player. Chairs are best but you can also use hoops, cushions or mats.

How to play

The aim of the game is players to work as a team and prevent the alien from sitting in a chair. The alien can only walk and the rest can run. The leader should go first so that they can demonstrate the game. To begin, the leader is 'the alien' and places their chair in the space but does not sit on it. The alien starts on the opposite side of the space from his empty chair. The rest of the players are seated on their chairs.

The alien walks towards the empty chair. He must walk not run, the slower the better. As he walks towards the chair any player can move from their seat and run to sit in it. As soon as a player moves from their chair it becomes free for the alien to sit on, but another player must prevent the alien from sitting down by getting there first. For the first few games, the alien should walk very slowly to allow the players to understand how to work together to prevent him from sitting in a chair.

If the alien manages to sit in a chair the last person in that chair is the new alien. That chair becomes the empty chair for the start of the new game. The new alien must start on the opposite side of the room from the empty chair and walk towards it. The person who is the alien will change many times in this game. Once a player leaves a chair they cannot go back to it until they have sat in another chair first.

65. Giants, witches and elves

Age range: 10–12
Players: 10 or more
Set up time: 1–2 minutes
Playing time: 5–10 minutes
Formation: Create two 'safe' zones 8 metres apart.
Space: A large room, hall or outside on the grass.

How to play

Before starting, teach the players how to become the three different characters of giant, witch and elf. Each character has a motion and sound.

The Characters

The giant – Stand on your tippy toes, arms in the air and make a loud 'Roooar' noise.

The witch – Ride an imaginary broomstick and make a cackling 'He he he' laugh.

The elf – Bend forward, cupping hands over ears and make a high-pitched 'Eiieee' noise.

The giant beats the elf through strength.

The witch beats the giant with spells.

The elf beats the witch with their cleverness.

Practise the characters a few times together while reminding the group which character beats which. Divide the group into two teams and have them stand in their safety zone. Each team huddles together and as a group secretly decides on one character. Everyone on a team must all play the same character. When both teams have chosen their characters, they walk into the middle of the space and stand in a line facing each other about two feet apart. On the count of 3 or the words 'Abracadabra' the members of both teams must play their character at the same time. Members of the team who choose the winning character must chase and tip as many players on the opposite team before they can run back to their safety zone. Players that are tipped must join the other team. Play many times and watch how the size of the groups continue to change.

66. Mr/Ms Hit

Age range: 10–12
Players: 6 or more
Set up time: 1–3 minutes – needs to be explained well
Playing time: 5–15 minutes
Formation: Define the play boundaries in a large playing area.
Space: Enough room to run around in. Can be indoors or outdoors.

How to play

Allow plenty of time to teach this game before you start.

This is a version of tip. One person is 'Mr/Ms Hit'. Mr Hit begins by chasing a player. The player who is being chased avoids being tipped by quickly calling out another player's name. The person whose name is called immediately becomes the new Mr Hit. The new Mr Hit then chases or tips any player and the old Mr Hit becomes a player. To save yourself from being tipped you must call out the name of another player in the game.

If a player is tipped before they can call another player's name, they are out. The player who is out leaves the game, and the player who got them out continues on as Mr Hit. Mr Hit can only chase one player at a time to avoid confusion. Players are out if:
* If Mr Hit tips them before they call out another player's name.
* If they call out the name of a player who is already out.
* If they go outside the boundaries.

67. Cyclone

Age range: 10–12
Players: 5 or more
Playing time: 1–2 minutes
Formation: Standing in a circle holding each other's wrists.
Space: A large area indoors or outdoors that is clear of obstacles.

How to play

Clear the area of obstacles. Ask the players to join together by holding their neighbour by the wrists, monkey grip style. Place an empty cardboard box or a chair in the middle of the circle of players. The aim is to push or pull any player so that they touch the object in the middle. If they touch the object they leave the circle and players rejoin their grip. If a player breaks their grip they also leave the circle. Play until there is only one player left who has not touched the object or broken their grip. This player is declared the winner.

Safety:
This is a very physical game. Ask players to be careful and be mindful of each other so as not to cause an injury.

68. Knee fencing

Age range: 10–12
Players: 2 or more – even numbers
Set up time: 1–2 minutes
Playing time: 5–10 minutes
Formation: Children form pairs and stand about 50 centimetres away from each other.
Space: Fairly large; 8–10 metres

How to play

This game is fast and fun. It is a physical contact game and should be played with care. When the leader calls 'Go', partners try to tip each other's knees and avoid being tipped on the knee by their partner. The first player to tip their partner's knee three times wins. Tell the players to be careful of bumping heads.

To extend the game, winners can player winners until there is one winner left. Those not playing can help adjudicate, by standing in a circle around the players who are in.

This is a good game to play in a circle whereby one (or two) pairs play the game in the centre of the circle while the group watches. Playing it in a circle makes the game more theatrical.

Variation

Toe fencing

Players pair up and hold hands. On 'Go,' they try to step lightly on each other's toes while avoiding having their own toes stepped on. First to three wins.

69. Pushing back to back

Age range: 10–12
Players: 6 or more
Set up time: 1–2 minutes
Playing time: 5 minutes
Formation: Players of equal size stand in a line, back to back in the middle of the room.
Space: 8–10 metres required and this game needs to be played on a soft surface such as grass or mats.

How to play

The partners link elbows and lean into each other's lower backs with knees slightly bent, making sure that their lower backs are touching. (The lower back is around where your pants sit on your hips.)

On 'Go', partners push against their opponent's back and shift them to the other side of the room. Players must remain on their feet. The player who can push their opponent to the other side of the room is the winner. This is a physical contact exercise and should be played sensibly. If players fall down they can get up and continue.

Back to back race

Ask players to choose a partner. Each pair stands back to back with their arms linked but sideways in a line. Pairs line up behind a start line. On the word 'Go' each pair runs sideways with their arms linked to a finish line. First pair to reach the finish line wins.

Back to back relay

Divide players into two teams and have them choose a partner. Each couple stands back to back with arms linked but standing sideways in a line. The two teams line up in two lines behind a start line. On the word 'Go' each couple runs sideways to a goal line and back. The first team to finish, with all players sitting down, wins.

70. Sock tag

Age range: 10–12
Players: 5 or more
Set up time: 1–2 minutues
Playing time: 5–10 minutes
Formation: Random chasing.
Space: A large space either indoors or outdoors.
Materials: Socks, or enough scraps of material for each player, such as scarves, tea tow

How to play

Set the play boundaries. Everyone tucks a sock or scarf into the back of their pants so that it looks like a short tail.

Players run around within the play boundaries trying to steal each other's socks, whilst avoiding their own sock being stolen. If a player steals your sock, you are out. The winner is the last person to lose their sock or the last person left with a sock still tucked in their pants.

Speed it up

You can speed up the game by keeping the players who get out involved. Players who lose their socks may stand on the boundary lines and remove other player's socks if they come near them. They must not move their feet.

Variation

If you steal a player's sock you can keep that sock in case your own is taken. If your sock is taken you may use the sock you stole as a back up and remain in game by tucking the stolen sock into the back of your pants. You can continue to use stolen socks as back up socks until you have none left. When you have none left you are out. The winner is the last player with a sock still tucked into the back of their pants.

Variation

Ground version

This version of the game needs to be played on a soft surface, such as on grass or mats. Players start on the ground with their socks pulled off their heels but still over their toes. Players crawl around on their hands and knees and steal each other's socks from their feet. Once both socks are stolen a player is out. Players can't keep back-up socks. The last person wearing a sock wins.

71. Toe jump

Age range: 5 and up
Players: 4 or more
Setup time: 2 minutes
Playing time: 5–15 minutes
Formation: Scattered running.
Space: A largish area needed around 10 by 10 metres.

How to play

Give each player a number to remember. All stand in a circle with one arm straight out touching fingers in the middle. When the leader calls 'Go', all players jump away from one another. Each player then takes turns initiating a jump. The first person to jump is player number 1. They try to jump lightly on the toes of any player. As player number 1 jumps all the other players jump at the same time. Players jump to either get away or to get someone out. Play continues with player number 2 jumping and so on. Any player can jump on any other player's toes as long as they jump when it is either their go or when the person whose go it is jumps. As players get out skip their go. The winner of the game is the last person left in. For safety, remind players not to land too heavily on other players' toes and also make sure that this is played in bare feet or all the players have similar footwear. If you think that some children are having trouble with the game, leave this game out.

There are a number of ways to get out.

- ★ If someone jumps/lands on your toes.
- ★ If the initiator fakes a jump and a player leaves the ground or over balances.
- ★ If you jump out of turn.
- ★ If you don't jump on your turn.

72. Limbo

Age range: 10–12
Players: 5 or more
Set up time: 5 minutes
Playing time: 2–20 minutes
Formation: In a line.
Space: Can be played in a small space.
Materials: A wooden broom or a light plastic pole about 4–5 metres long.
Lively and upbeat music.

How to play

This is based on a dance that originated in Trinidad and people of all ages can play this game. Two people hold a long pole or broom at each end at about shoulder height. One at a time, players must dance or go under the pole by leaning backwards. They must not touch the pole with any part of their body nor put their hands on the ground.

Once all players have successfully moved under the pole, the pole-holders lower the pole slightly. The players go again in single file dancing or walking under the pole without bending forward or touching the pole. Any player who touches the pole or places their hands on the floor is out. Lower the height of the pole a little each time around. The last player in wins.

If you play this game with small children, they can move under the pole without touching it or putting their hands on the ground.

73. Imaginary ball

Age range: 10–12
Players: 5 or more
Set up time: Under a minute
Playing time: 2–3 minutes
Formation: Standing in a circle facing inwards.
Space: Can be played in a small space either indoors or outdoors.

How to play

Throw a pretend ball around the circle. Encourage players to believe in the existence of the imaginary ball and be creative with different throws. Play with the idea of different types of balls, such as a bowling ball, a balloon, a tennis ball or a football, allowing players to experiment with weight and speed.

For example, the leader may start by throwing an imaginary tennis ball. Allow it to be passed back and forth around the circle. The leader may then suggest that it is a bowling ball and the players must pass it as such around the circle. After a while the leader may suggest that it is a balloon. As players become more familiar with the exercise they can start making the changes without instructions at any time they like. Finally introduce the idea of making a sound each time they throw the ball.

There is no right or wrong way of throwing in this exercise. The more creative the children are the better.

74. Bang!

Age range: 5 and up
Players: 4 or more
Setup time: 2 minutes
Playing time: 5-15 minutes
Formation: Scattered running
Space: A largish area needed around 10 by 10 metres.

How to play

One person is in and stands in the middle of the circle. They turn around on the spot and quickly shoot one of the players, by making a gun with their hands and forefingers and saying the word 'BANG!'. If you are concerned with the use of the 'gun' imagery, change this to 'Splat' (see variation opposite).

The player who is shot at, ducks and the players standing either side shoot at one another and say 'BANG'! The fastest player stays in the game. The player who is out sits down in their spot. If in doubt, the person in the middle decides. The player who ducked stands back up. If both players BANG! at the same time then it is a tie and they both stay in the game.

The person in the middle continues to spin around and say BANG! to people in the circle. As more people get out it becomes harder for the players to work out who is shooting at who. Play until only two players are left.

Use an imaginary duel (spaghetti western-style) to decide the winner. Ask the two remaining players to stand back to back. The

134

shooter calls 'Walk' and they walk away from one another until the shooter calls 'GO' and the players turn, shoot and say 'BANG!'. The fastest play wins.

Variation

Splat!

Play the game in the same way but the person in the middle points to a player and calls out 'Splat!' The person they pointed at must duck and the two people either side must splat each other by pointing at each other and calling out 'Splat!' The last one to do so is out. Continue until there are only two players left in the circle. Determine the winner with the imaginary duel but players point and say 'Splat!'

75. Knife and fork

Age range: 7–9 and 10–12
Players: 6 or more
Set up time: 1–2 minutes
Playing time: 5–15 minutes
Formation: Players pair up and stand randomly around the play space.
Space: Enough space for the players to move around.

How to play

This is a good game to play after Giant letters on p.64. The leader calls out a description of two things that go together, such as 'Knife and fork'. Without talking, one partner chooses to make part of the image with their body. For example, if they choose to be the knife they stand tall with their arms in the air. Their partner accepts their offer and makes the shape of the fork with their body by standing with their arms in the air bent at the elbows. There is no right or wrong 'shape' as it is open to the player's imagination. Give the players plenty of time to find their positions.

When a player offers a shape their partner must match their offer by working with them. The pairs hold their position (frozen) until the leader calls out another description. The leader can point out a particular pair with an interesting/creative or funny image to the group. Pairs must get into positions as quickly as possible without talking.

Some suggestions to call out:
* Flower in a vase.
* That same flower three weeks later.
* Needle and thread.
* Cup and saucer.
* A pair of jeans. The two players can be a leg each.
* A pair of wet jeans. The two players will make their bodies look floppy and drippy.
* A foot in a shoe. One player makes a shoe with their body such as lying on the floor curled up. The other player stands in the middle of them.
* A bowl of spaghetti: similar to above, one player makes the bowl with their body such as curling up on the floor. The other player turns their body into spaghetti (arms and legs akimbo) while standing or lying between the first player.
* Baby in a cradle.
* A racing car and driver.

Some less obscure suggestions are:
* Eye and contact lenses.
* Bowl and spoon.
* Pencil and a pencil sharpener.
* Table and chair.

137

76. Postcards

Age range: 10–12
Players: 8 or more
Set up time: 1–3 minutes
Playing time: 5–15 minutes
Formation: Players get into groups of four and randomly stand around the play space.
Space: Enough space for the players to move around.

How to play

This is a good game to follow from 'Knife and Fork' as the pairs can link up with another pair. Players use their bodies physically to make up a scene that is described by the leader.

The leader calls out 'at the beach'. Players create an image of a beach scene. For example, one person might be a wave, another is the surfboard and the third person is surfing. They must hold this scene still until the next one is called. The leader calls out 'dinner at home' and one person might be the table, someone else is eating and the third person is serving food. Once the groups are in their scenes allow time for everyone to see what others have done.

138

Examples to call out

* In a hospital.
* In the classroom.
* At the zoo.
* At the ballet.
* At the circus.
* The first day of school.
* In the library.

Variation

To do this exercise players form random groups each time. Ask the players to walk about the space. The leader calls a number and a scene. For example, the leader calls '4' and 'skydiving'. In silence, 4 players group together and quickly make the frozen image of people skydiving. The leader calls 'Walk' and the groups dissolve and players go back to walking. Next the leader calls out the number 2 and 'Washing the car'. Quickly players in the group pair up and create a frozen image of washing the car. Play as many times as you like, calling different numbers and descriptions. You can be as descriptive as you like such as painting a

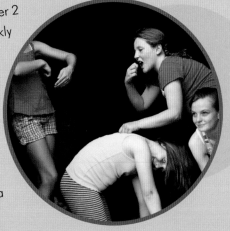

77. Expert double figures

Age range: 7–9 and 10–12
Players: 8; 4 plus an audience
Set up time: 2–5 minutes
Playing time: 5–10 minutes
Formation: Standing in a circle facing inwards.
Space: This game can be played in a small space.
Materials: Two chairs and plenty of imagination.

How to play

Select two pairs of players while the rest of the group looks on. Within the two pairs decide who will play the 'talking heads', and who will play the 'hands'. The talking heads sit side by side in a chair facing the front. They hold their hands behind their backs. The children who play the 'hands' stand (or kneel) behind the talking heads and slide their arms under the arms of the talking heads so it looks like their hands belong to the talking heads.

Decide who will be the interviewer. One of the talking heads interviews the other and the people who play the 'hands' pretend to be their hands as they discuss a topic. Give the interviewer a question such as 'Doctor Watkins, tell me about your new flying invention'. He or she interviews their partner and as they discuss the new invention the 'hands' make gestures to go with the conversation.

Interview suggestions

* Today we have the amazing singer (player's name) in our studio. Tell me how you became a singer and formed your band.
* Tell me about your last holiday.
* I hear you have created a new robot that cleans the house. How does it work?
* I hear that you have just developed a car that drives itself? Can you tell us more about it?

78. What are you doing?

Age range: 7–9 and 10–12
Players: 6 or more
Set up time: 1–3 minutes
Playing time: 3 minutes
Formation: Standing in a circle facing inwards.
Space: This game can be played in a small space.

How to play

The leader begins by miming an action in the centre of the circle. They may start with a mime of hanging the washing on the line, for example. After a few moments, any player can step forward and ask them 'What are you doing?' The leader who is miming must freeze. They answer with a description of another action based on the physical position they are in. For example, if they are standing with their arms in the air, they may reply 'I am escaping through the window'. The player who asked the question swaps positions and starts miming an escape through the window. At any time, a player may ask 'what are you doing?', and the game continues. Players can ask and mime as many times as they like.

Players should not actively think of an action rather let their physical position they are in when asked the question 'what are you doing' inform them of the next action. Allow the players to have fun with miming and give them time to explore and be creative.

79. Charades

Age range: 10–12 (or children of a range of ages working together)
Players: 4 or more.
Set up time: 10 minutes
Playing time: 30 minutes or longer
Formation: Some people perform for others while they sit and watch.
Space: Indoors with plenty of space to sit and watch the game.
Materials: Stopwatch, pen, paper, hat and a good imagination.

How to play

Charades is a pantomime game. Players act out a word or phrase without speaking and their team members guess what it is. The aim of the game is to guess the answer as quickly as possible.

Divide players into two teams. Have ready-made titles of movies, books or TV shows written on pieces of paper. Make sure you choose titles that are appropriate for the age and ability of the players. Do not allow players to see these titles. Choose well-known titles that can be acted out. Place the pieces of paper in a hat. One member of the first team picks a title from the hat. After a few minutes to think about the title, they must act out that title in silence to their team members.

The player must first indicate what category it is, such as movie, book or TV show. Next they indicate how many words are in the title by holding up the number of fingers. They then indicate which word they want to start to act out first by holding up that number of fingers again. Once a word is guessed correctly they move onto another.

continued overleaf

Team members call out the answers. Once the correct answer is called the player indicates that they are right by pointing at their nose with one hand and pointing to the person who called out the right answer with the other hand. This is 'On the nose'. See below for all hand signals.

If their team members don't guess the correct title in three minutes you can call 'time's up' and they have to sit down. It is then the next team's turn.

If a word is difficult the player can break it up into syllables and act out syllables of the word to create the entire word. By guessing the syllables the team will then work out the entire word and move onto the next word.

The game continues until each player has had a chance to act out a title. The team that guessed correctly most often wins. If the teams are guessing correctly within the 3 minutes you will need to time their goes so that the team who is the overall fastest wins.

Hand signals

Categories
Movie title: Pretend to crank an old-fashion movie camera.
Book title: Fold and unfold your hands as if they are a book.
TV show: Draw a rectangle to outline the TV screen.
Song title: Pretend to sing.
Play title: Pretend to pull the rope that opens a theatre curtain.

Word Signs that have to be done to make sense of the phrase or title
Number of words in the title: Hold up the number of fingers.
Which word you're working on: Hold up the number of fingers again.
Number of syllables in the word: Lay the number of fingers on your forearm.
Which syllable you're working on: Lay the number of fingers on your upper arm again.

Length of word: Bring your hands together or wide apart as though indicating the size of a fish.

Other hand signals

Yes, that's right: Point at their nose with one hand and point to the person who called out the right answer with the other hand.

Sounds like: Cup one hand behind an ear. Mime the word it sounds like. Players must then shout out rhyming words until they get it right.

Longer version of: Pretend to stretch a piece of elastic.

Shorter version of: Do a 'karate chop' with your hand.

Little word: Bring your thumb and index fingers close together. The people guessing call out every little word they can think of ('on, in, the, and') until you gesticulate wildly to indicate the right word.

The: Make the letter T with your fingers.

Close, keep guessing!: Frantically wave hands to keep the guesses coming.

Plural: Link your little fingers.

Past tense: Wave your hand over your shoulder towards your back.

The entire concept: Sweep your arms through the air.

Variation

Non-competitive
Alternatively, you can play for fun and not worry about timing the teams. You may also choose pairs or individuals to play to the group as a whole and everyone tries to guess.

80. Leading the blind

Age range: 10–12
Players: 6 or more
Set up time: 1 minute
Playing time: 5–6 minutes
Formation: Players are paired up and move around the space randomly.
Space: This game can be played in a small space.

How to play

This is a good exercise for creating awareness of the space around and for building trust. A leader in each partnership is chosen and holds their hand out at the elbow with their palm facing up. The other partner places their hand on top of the leader's with their palm facing down.

The leader asks their partner to close their eyes. The leader slowly walks forward and the partner moves with the leader, keeping their eyes closed. The leader must start slowly to develop trust, taking small steps and moving with caution at all times. As trust and confidence grows the leader can begin to change direction, go backwards, increase the walking speed or even go up steps.

Ask the 'blind partner' to be aware of their other senses. They will begin to focus on sound and light in order to get their bearings and they will become more aware of temperature and breezes within the space. After a number of minutes swap over.

Step 2

Play again with the same partners but this time ask them to only touch finger tips. The leader walks their partner around the space. Then swap over.

Step 3

Play again with the same partners but this time the leader only uses their voice to guide their partner around the space. There is no physical contact between them. The leader uses their voice by giving commands and offering encouragement to ensure that their partner moves safely about the room with their eyes closed. Swap around.

80. Silent detective

Age range: 10–12
Players: 10 or more
Playing time: 3–7 minutes
Formation: Walking randomly in the space with eyes closed.
Space: An area of 10 by 10 metres either indoors or outdoors. Set the playing boundaries.

How to play

Clear the area of obstacles and divide the group in half. One half of the group is the guardians and they stand at the edges of the play boundaries to protect the players.

The first half of the group stand anywhere within the play area and close their eyes. The games leader moves around the group and taps one player on the head. That player is the silent detective. The games leader asks the players to turn around three times. On the words 'go' players move off, walking slowly within the play area with their eyes closed. Players and guardians remain silent. The guardians stand on the edges and protect the players from walking out of the play area or harming themselves by gently turning them in the right directions.

Players walk slowly and carefully. If they bump into another player they move aside to pass. The silent detective's aim is to catch all the players. If the silent detective bumps into a player they take their hand. That player stays joined to the silent detective and if they touch another player they take their hand thus forming a chain of captured players. Only players on either end of the chain can use their free hand to capture another player. Play in this way until all players have linked hands. Swap around so the guardians become players and vice versa.

82. Two-finger lift

Age range: 10–12
Players: 8 or more
Set up time: 1 minute
Playing time: 5–6 minutes
Formation: This game involves the whole group as a team.
Space: This game can be played in a small space

How to play

One player lies very still on their back. The rest of the group positions themselves around the player on the floor next to their waist, upper legs, upper arms and head. The players place their index and middle fingers under their team-mate's body and together begin to lift the person off the floor. Players must use two hands but only use two fingers. For an effective lift you require at least three players either side and one player at the head of their team mate.

   The team will be amazed that they can lift a member of their group in this way. Make sure they only lift the player to a height they are comfortable with and place them back on the floor gently. Swap around so that everyone has a turn. This can also be done sitting down with fingers under the armpits and knees.

83. Circle of trust

Age range: 10 – 12
Players: 10 or more
Set up time: 1 minute
Playing time: 5–6 minutes
Formation: Standing in a circle facing inwards.
Space: This game can be played in a small space.

How to play

You may choose to do this exercise in same sex groups if it is more appropriate. One person stands in the middle of the circle. All the others make a tight circle around them, standing back by about 60 cm. The player in the middle folds their arms across their chest. Keeping their feet in the same spot at all times, the person in the middle gently tips forward into the hands of the players in the circle, falling about 15 to 20 degrees. People in the circle have their hands held up at chest height to support and stop their team member from falling on the ground. Two or three people will 'catch' the middle person at a time. They will gently rock the middle person back across to the other side of the circle where other players 'catch' them. Players can also pass the person in the middle around the circle. The middle person must not move their feet, and keep their body rigid.

Always be very aware of how comfortable people are with this exercise as it can be quite confronting for some.

84. Twenty-one

Age range: 7–9 and 10–12
Players: 10 or more
Set up time: 1 minute
Playing time: 5 minutes
Formation: Sitting in a circle facing inwards.
Space: This game can be played in a small space.

How to play

This is a good game for bringing a group back together as it encourages focus and concentration. The aim of the game is to count to 21 as a group. No two players can say the same number at once. The leader starts by calling out the number 1. Any player can then call out 2. If they say the number by themselves then any player can call out 3. Proceed in this manner until reaching 21. If two people say the same number at once then start again at number 1. A player cannot call out two numbers in a row.

85. Riddle treasure hunt

Age range: 10–12 (or children of varying ages working together)
Players: 3 or more
Set up time: Approximately 30–60 minutes
Playtime: Around 30 minutes, may be longer
Formation: Children work in a group searching for clues and hiding spots around the house or outside.
Space: Indoors or outdoors.
Materials: Pen and paper, riddles, and the Treasure (chocolates, a present, tickets to a concert).

Setting up

Write down 10 or more riddles on cardboard or paper. Choose easy or more difficult clues depending on the group. Hide the treasure first and keep the clue that leads to the treasure to the side. Chose one clue to be the starting clue. Decide how you will present the first clue to the players (see opposite). Now hide all the other clues so one leads to the other. The last clue you hide is the one that leads to the treasure. Keep a list of where you have hidden each clue and the order they are in.

How to play

You can start the treasure hunt many different ways. For a simple start, write the first clue on a piece of card, cut it into pieces and place it in an envelop that you give to the players. They must put the card together to read the clue. You can do this for all clues so they have to complete the puzzle before they can read the clue. Be as creative as you like.

Give the children the first clue. The children read the first clue and guess the answer, which will lead them to a place in the house or garden. There you will have hidden the next clue, which they will find and it will lead to the next clue and so on. The final clue leads to the treasure.

* It is very cold in here = the freezer/fridge.

* Where clothes go when you have worn them = laundry (basket).

* The car (or bikes) are kept in here = carport, garage.

* I use it to get clean = bath or shower.

* I use it to leave the house = front door, door mat.

* I use it every night before I go to bed = toothbrush (holder).

* I wear them running = a pair of joggers.

* People send me messages here = letterbox or PC.

Examples

Other more difficult clues (riddles)

- I show my true colours in Spring = flowers.
- What has no wings but flies? = the garbage bin.
- What runs around a yard but never moves? = the fence.
- What has no legs but runs? = a tap.
- What has five fingers but no nails? = a glove.
- What has two legs but can't walk? = a pair of pants.

Skipping and ball games

86. Learning to skip

Age range: All ages
Players: 10 or more
Set up time: 2 minutes
Playing time: 5–30 minutes
Formation: Two players hold a 5–7 metre rope at either end. Swap regularly so that everyone gets a go.
Space: Outdoors or in a large room/hall.
Materials: A length of rope around 5 metres or more in length. The larger the group the longer the rope should be.

How to play

Skipping is a great group activity as a physical warm-up. It is lots of fun and helps with coordination, timing and fitness. To help younger children learn to skip, start with two people holding the rope and swinging it from side to side so that the skipper can jump over the rope easily. The following skipping games are group games with two people turning the rope for the players.

87. Run through the rope

Two people turn the rope in full circles. Players line up on one side of the rope. One at a time, players run under the turning rope without jumping and out again. They run around the back of the rope holder and line up on the other side ready to go again. The pattern makes a figure 8 around the two rope turners as the 'skippers' run through the turning rope continuously. Encourage the players to run through leaving no gaps in between the next person (that is, if the rope touches the ground and no-one has passed through).

88. Link arms

Players link arms at the elbows and run through in pairs. Do a full figure 8 so they get to go twice each. Now ask players to link arms in threes and go again. Try for 4, 5 until everyone is together. See if players can run through all in one group with their arms linked.

89. Jump over

Two people turn the rope in full circles. Players line up on one side of the rope. One at a time, players run into the turning rope, they jump once over the rope and run out again. They run around the back of the rope holder and line up on the other side ready to go again. The pattern makes a figure 8 around the two rope turners.

Ask the players to link arms and jump over the rope with their arms linked. Try building up the groups to see how many people can run in with their arms linked together successfully to jump the rope and run out without tripping up.

90. Birthday game

There are many songs and rhymes for skipping games. Here are a few to get started. Two people turn the rope in full circles. Players line up on one side of the rope. Skippers jump into the turning rope when their birthday month is called. Eventually, all skippers will be skipping together. As their birthday date is called they jump back out.

The rhyme goes as follows:

'All in together
Never mind the weather
When I call your birthday (month)
You must jump in.'

'January, February,
March, April,
May, June,
July, August
September, October
November, December'

160

'All out together
it's mighty fine weather
when it's your birthday (date)
please jump out
1, 2, 3, 4, 5, etc. to 31'

So if you were born on 16 January. You jump in on the month of January and stay skipping while all the other months are called and all the other players jump into the turning rope. When the number 16 is called you jump out. If someone trips up then stop the rope, ask all players to stand on one side of the rope and continue the chant where you left off.

91. Teddy bear

Players take turns skipping. While everyone chants the rhyme, skippers must do the actions while the rope is above their heads. At the end of the rhyme the first skipper jumps out and the next one comes in. The rhyme starts again for each new skipper. If a skipper steps on the rope or misses an action, then they are out. Players who are out take over turning the rope. You can play Teddy bear in pairs or groups so that two or more people are in at once.

The song

'Teddy Bear, Teddy Bear turn around
(the skipper turns around)
Teddy Bear, Teddy Bear touch the ground
(the skipper touches the ground)

continued overleaf

161

Teddy Bear, Teddy Bear tie your shoe
(the skipper pretends to tie their shoelace)
Teddy Bear, Teddy Bear that will do!
Teddy Bear, Teddy Bear climb the stairs
(the skipper pretends to climb stairs)
Teddy Bear, Teddy Bear say your prayers
(the skipper puts the hands together)
Teddy Bear, Teddy Bear turn off the lights
(the skipper pretends to switch off the light)
Teddy Bear, Teddy Bear say good night'
(the skipper runs out from the rope and waves good bye)

92. One, two, three, fast skipping

One person stands in the middle of the rope. The rope turners turn the rope at normal speed for 3 jumps then they turn the rope twice as fast to see how long the skipper can stay in. When playing with a group count the number of jumps each player managers at fast speed. The player with the most jumps wins. If you are using a heavy skipping rope be careful of hitting the legs or head of the skipper as it can hurt.

93. Under and overs

Age range: 7–9, 10–12
Players: 10 or more
Set up time: 1–3 minutes
Playing time: 5–10 minutes
Formation: Two teams in a line.
Space: Outdoors or in a hall.
Materials: At least two balls for one per team, either a netball or a soccer ball.

How to play

Divide the group into two teams of 4–5 people. Ask the players of each team to line up one behind the other in the same direction in single file. The front players begin with a ball each. They pass the ball between their legs to the player behind them. The second player then passes the ball over their head to the player behind them. Repeat this under and over pattern until the ball reaches the end of the line. The last player takes the ball and runs to the front of the line with all other players shuffling back slightly. Repeat this process until all players return to their original starting position. The first team to return to their starting position wins.

94. Ball partners

Age range: 7–9, 10–12
Players: 2 or more
Set up time: 1–2 minutes
Playing time: 3–5 minutes
Formation: Players group in pairs.
Space: Indoors or outdoors.
Materials: One ball per pair – a soft ball the size of a netball or soccer ball.
You can use a tennis ball but it's just a little trickier.

How to play

This is a simple partner exercise. Give each pair a ball. Ask them to work together to keep the ball between them without using their hands. They may support the ball between their backs and then move around so the ball moves to balance between their shoulders and so on. Ask the pairs to find as many different positions with the ball between them without letting the ball drop to the ground.

95. Fifty-one up

Age range: 10–12
Players: 4 or more
Set up time: 1–2 minutes
Playing time: 5–10 minutes
Formation: Standing in a loose circle.
Space: Best played outside or in a hall with a high ceiling.
Materials: A beach ball or soft ball.

How to play

This is a good focus game. Using a ball, the group task is to keep the ball in the air for 51 counts without letting it touch the ground. One person lightly throws the ball into the air and everyone counts out '1', another player must tap the ball back into the air before it touches the group and the group counts '2' and so on. No one can touch the ball twice in a row. If the ball falls to the ground a player picks it up and the counting begins at 1 again. Continue until the group reaches 51 or tires. It is best to hit the ball lightly with your fingertips and open palms.

96. Ball tag

Age range: 7–9, 10–12
Players: 5 or more
Set up time: 1–2 minutes
Playing time: 5–7 minutes
Formation: Running randomly within the playing boundaries.
Space: A large area either outdoors or in a hall.
Materials: A tennis ball or juggling ball.

How to play

Two people are in. Their aim is to tip people but they can only tip other players when in possession of the ball. They must stand still when holding the ball and reach their hands out as far as possible to tip other players. The two people who are in pass the ball between them whilst moving around the group but they must stay on one spot when holding the ball. Once a player is tipped they become in and throw and catch the ball to help to tip other players. The winner is the last person to be tipped. If the two people who are in can't catch anyone out, choose another person to be in to assist them.

97. Balloon chin relay

Age range: 7–9, 10–12
Players: 4 or more
Playing time: 5 – 7 minutes
Formation: Two teams lined up side by side in a single file, facing the same direction.
Space: A large area–outdoors or in a hall
Materials: One balloon per team or very soft balls (blow the balloon up to half its normal size).

How to play

Place a marker about 5–10 metres from the front of each line. The first player in each team places the balloon under their chin.

When the leader shouts 'Go!' or blows the whistle the players must run around the marker and back with the balloon under their chin. If the balloon slips they must pick it up, place it back under their chin and start from where it fell.

Once they have run around the marker the first team member positions the balloon under the chin of the next player without using their hands. The first player goes to the end of the line. The next player runs around the marker and back. They then pass the balloon to the next player without using their hands.

Each team member runs once, but if the teams are uneven select a player to run twice (such as at the start and then at the end). A team wins when all players have run once and sits down first with their balloon still intact.

98. Captain ball

Age range: 7–9 and 10–12
Players: 8 or more
Set up time: 1–3 minutes
Playing time: 5–10 minutes
Formation: Two teams standing in two straight lines.
Space: A marker for where the Captain stands.
Materials: One ball per team, such as a netball or soccer ball.

How to play

Line up both teams in a single file facing the front. The captain of each team stands 1–2 metres away from the first person on the team. On the signal the captain throws the ball to the first player in the line who returns the ball and sits down. The captain throws the ball to the next player who returns the ball and sits down. The captain throws the ball to each player in turn. The last player catches the ball and runs to the position of the captain.

The captain joins the front of the line. All players stand up and shuffle back. Repeat this process until all players have had a turn. The first team to complete a full round and finishes all sitting down wins.

99. Tunnel ball

Age range: 7–9, 10–12
Players: 10 or more
Set up time: 1–3 minutes
Playing time: 5–10 minutes
Formation: Two teams standing in two straight lines.
Space: Outdoors or in a hall.
Materials: One ball per team, such as a netball or soccer ball.

How to play

All players on each team line up in a straight line facing the same direction with their legs standing apart. The player at the end of the line turns to face the other way and stands with their knees bent and their head down looking for the ball as it comes through the legs. When the signal is given, the two players at the front of each line rolls the ball through the legs of their team members. Once the ball has made it to the end, that player picks up the ball and runs to the start of the line and proceeds to roll the ball. The new end player turns and waits for the ball to come through. This is continued until everyone has had a turn. The first team to complete a full round so that all players have a turn and then sits downs wins.

100. Hand ball

Age range: 7–9, 10–12
Players: 4 (or more)
Set up time: 5–7 minutes
Playing time: 5–30 minutes
Formation: Players in pairs facing each other.
Space: In the school yard or in a gym or hall.
Materials: A tennis ball and a hard surface such as concrete or wooden floors

This is your traditional school-yard handball which you can play in a group or the kids can play in groups of four.

Set up

Use chalk to mark out four squares on the ground. All four squares touch each other to make one large square. Each square is roughly 3 by 3 metres/8 by 8 feet but they can be bigger if desired. Each player occupies a square. Each square has a rank order. The highest rank is 'King' then 'Queen', 'Prince', then 'Joker'.

How to play

To start the game, the king serves the ball by bouncing it in his square once, then hitting it into one of the other players' squares. The receiving player then hits the ball into the square of any player, but they must first bounce it in their own square. If the ball bounces in a player's square they must hit it or they are out.

A player who is out moves into the lowest ranking square and all other players move up to fill the gap. You can play this game with more than four and the extra players wait on the side-line. Players who get out go to the side-line and the person at the front of the line moves onto the lowest ranking square to play. This game can be played with four squares in a line.

Note

A player is out if:

* A player fails to hit a ball that has bounced into their square.
* If the player hits a ball that lands on a line.
* A player hits the ball anywhere other than into the square of another player, that is, out of bounds.
* If the ball bounces more than once in a player's square before they hit it.
* If a player calls out 'challenge' to another player, they play continuously until one player is out according to the above list.

Game combinations for groups of players

Below is a list of games that work well together for a session that will last around 30 minutes to an hour depending on how large the group is. Please note that games such as charades, treasure hunts and limbo can last up to an hour on their own depending on the size of the group and the commitment of the players.

Just for fun
for 5–6 year olds
Colour and action
Pass the hoop
Duck, duck, goose
Stuck in the mud
River, bank, bridge
Red light, green light
Musical chairs

Party games
for 5–6 year olds
Follow the leader
Musical statues
Snake rope
Balloon tennis (inside only)
Egg and spoon race
Apple bobbing
Treasure hunt

Draw a hopscotch course for kids to use

Outdoor games
for 5–6 year olds
Touch that
Stuck in the mud
Red light, green light
Octopus
River, bank, bridge
Chain tip
Snake rope
Skipping or ball games

Indoor games
for 5–6 year olds
One to ten
Musical statues
Hello
Heads down thumbs up
Chinese whispers
What am I?
Hide and seek or Fruit salad

Just for fun games
for 7–9 year olds
Name and action
Untie the knot
Captain's coming
The Simpsons
Dead ant
Cat and mouse
The Ha

Party games
for 7–9 year olds
Murder wink
Musical chairs
Sack race
Three-legged race
Spin the bottle in reverse
Tunnel ball
Balloon chin relay

Outdoor games
for 7–9 year olds
Name trow
Captain's coming
The Simpsons
Cat and mouse
Rock, paper, scissors
Tie stomp
Sack race
Three-legged race

Indoor games
for 7–9 year olds
Clap clap, click click
Secret leader
Murder wink
The hand game
Mirror
Musical chairs
Memory
Spin the bottle in reverse

More active games
for 7–9 year olds
River, bank, bridge
Red light, green light
Stuck in the mud
Rock, paper, scissors
The Simpsons
Under and overs
Tunnel ball
Balloon chin relays

Just for fun games
for 10–12 year olds
Line ups
Group juggle
Zip, zap, zoom
Giants, witches and elves
Mr/Ms Hit
Sock tag
The Ha

Party games
for 10–12 year olds
Giants, witches and elves
The chair game
Sock tag
Balloon chin relay
Limbo
Riddle treasure hunt or
Charades

Outdoor games for 10–12 year olds

Pirate raid
Giants, witches and elves
Knee fencing
Sock tag
Mr/Ms Hit
Skipping
Fifty-one up

Games for children (12 years and over) and adults

Line ups
Zip, zap, zoom
Group juggle
The chair game
Rock, paper, scissors
Cat and mouse
Scream

Indoor games for 10–12 year olds

Group juggle
Bang!
What are you doing?
Twenty-one
Limbo
Name throw
Charades

Drama for children (12 years and over) and adults

Bang!
Untie the knot
Giant letters
Knife and fork
Postcards
Expert double figures
The Ha

Drama games for 10–12 year olds

Zip, zap, zoom
The scream
Bang!
Giant letters
Knife and fork
Postcards
Expert double figures

Games to play at home with only 2 or 3 players

Memory game
Who am I?
Hide and seek
Balloon tennis
Photographic/riddle treasure hunt